HOW TO BE A
MANGA
ARTIST

First published in the United States of America in 2024 by
Thames & Hudson Inc., 500 Fifth Avenue, New York, New York 10110

How to be a Manga Artist © 2024 BesideBooks S.r.l, Italy

Text by Balthazar Pagani © 2024 BesideBooks S.r.l, Italy
Design by Bebung © 2024 BesideBooks S.r.l, Italy
Text and illustrations by Fumio Obata © 2024 Fumio Obata
Illustrations by Silvia Vanni © 2024 Silvia Vanni

Consultancy by Asuka Ozumi

Translated from the Italian by Edward Fortes

Library of Congress Control Number 2024933369

ISBN 978-0-500-66029-4

Printed and bound in China by Toppan Leefung Printing Limited

MIX
Paper | Supporting
responsible forestry
FSC® C104723

Be the first to know about our new releases,
exclusive content and author events by visiting
thamesandhudson.com
thamesandhudsonusa.com
thamesandhudson.com.au

HOW TO BE A MANGA ARTIST

BALTHAZAR PAGANI • AZUKA OSUMI

ILLUSTRATIONS BY
SILVIA VANNI

PRO TIPS BY
FUMIO OBATA

CONTENTS

WHAT IS MANGA?

Manga is the word used to describe comics (and graphic novels) created and developed in Japan—or those that come from outside Japan but use the techniques and language typically adopted by the Japanese comic book industry.

In the Japanese **kanji** writing system (which uses Chinese characters), the word manga is written like this:

漫画

The first character can be read with several different meanings, of which the main ones are UNRESTRICTED, CARICATURED, or WHIMSICAL. The second character simply means DRAWING or PICTURE.

The word "manga" first appeared in Japan as early as 1798, in the introduction to an illustrated book by the writer and illustrator Santō Kyōden. However, the term became more widespread from 1814 with the *Hokusai Manga*, a collection of caricatures and satirical sketches drawn by the famous painter Hokusai "in a free and light-hearted manner."

Since its beginnings as humble, unpretentious drawings—occasionally with the intention to mock or satirize—manga has come a long way. Today, Japan is the largest and most wide-ranging comic book market in the world: the vast number of options means you can find manga of any genre, on any subject.

You could talk about manga for hours, but defining exactly what a manga is can be more complicated than it seems. Saying a "Japanese comic" is correct, but also a bit reductive. This book will help you discover many of the features of manga: how they are created, a few tricks of the trade, and some of the major artists.

Do you want to be a manga artist? Then look no further . . . read on!

BALTHAZAR PAGANI

A BRIEF HISTORY OF MANGA

I imagine you're curious to find out more about manga—maybe you even talk about your favorite stories with your friends at school, or on social media? Just like you, Yoko and John love manga, and they've decided to find out how to become a **mangaka** (manga artist). But let's start from the beginning: join these two friends as they discover what manga is, and where the art form comes from . . .

ACTUALLY, FORMS OF ILLUSTRATED OR "GRAPHIC" NARRATIVE WERE ALREADY POPULAR IN JAPAN WELL BEFORE HOKUSAI. **E-MAKI**, FOR EXAMPLE, WERE STORIES TOLD THROUGH THE USE OF WORDS AND IMAGES, AND EITHER PAINTED OR PRINTED ON SCROLLS OF PAPER. SOME ELEMENTS RESEMBLE THE BALLOONS AND FLUID MOTION LINES WE FIND IN MANGA TODAY.

A CLEAR PRECURSOR TO MANGA DATES BACK TO 1862, WHEN THE ENGLISHMAN CHARLES WIRGMAN LAUNCHED *JAPAN PUNCH*, AN ILLUSTRATED SATIRICAL NEWSPAPER FOR ENGLISH EXPATRIATES LIVING IN JAPAN. SATIRICAL, SINGLE-PANEL CARTOONS EVENTUALLY FOUND AN AUDIENCE AMONG THE JAPANESE POPULATION AS WELL, UNDER THE NAME **PONCHI-E** (A DISTORTION OF "PUNCH") AND BEGAN TO APPEAR IN NATIONAL NEWSPAPERS.

THIS EXCHANGE WITH THE ANGLOPHONE WORLD KICKSTARTED THE DEVELOPMENT OF MANGA. YET THE TURNING POINT THAT MARKED THE MOVE BEYOND THE SATIRICAL, SINGLE-PANEL PONCHI-E CAME ABOUT THANKS TO IPPEI OKAMOTO, WHO INTRODUCED A WINNING INNOVATION TO THE *TOKYO SHIMBUN* DAILY NEWSPAPER IN 1912: A SEQUENCE OF FOUR PANELS. THIS LED TO THE BIRTH OF **YONKOMA** AND STORY-MANGA, THE POPULARITY OF WHICH SOON SURPASSED THAT OF THE SINGLE-PANEL PONCHI-E.

IN TIME, THE FOUR-PANEL FORMAT BECAME MORE COMPLEX. THIS WAS IN PART DUE TO THE DEMANDS OF POST-WAR READERS, WHO BEGAN TO PREFER STORIES WITH MORE INTRICATE, EPISODIC PLOTS. THIS CEMENTED THE POPULARITY OF STORY-MANGA AS WE KNOW IT TODAY.

OK, SO THERE'S **SHŌNEN**, AIMED AT BOYS.

THEY'RE LIKE STORIES OF FRIENDSHIP AND ADVENTURE, WITH LOTS OF ACTION.

EXAMPLES?

NARUTO, OR *DRAGON BALL*!

THEN THERE'S **SHŌJO**, AIMED AT GIRLS.

WHICH ARE OFTEN ROMANTIC STORIES, WITH MAGIC IN THEM . . .

WELL DONE! EXACTLY! HAVE YOU EVER READ ANY?

'COURSE MAN! WHO D'YOU TAKE ME FOR? THIS AIN'T 1960 ANYMORE . . .

YOU KNOW I'M A HUGE FAN OF *SAILOR MOON*!!!

HA HA, I KNOW! I WAS JUST JOKING! OK, MY TURN . . .

SO THEN THERE ARE **SEINEN**, WHICH ARE FOR ADULT MEN.

LIKE *TOKYO GHOUL* (WHICH I LOVE!)

. . . **JOSEI** FOR ADULT WOMEN, WHICH ARE ROMANCES . . .

. . . OR STORIES OF EVERYDAY LIFE LIKE *HAPPY MANIA*.

ALRIGHT EINSTEIN, DON'T GET DISTRACTED! WE GOTTA GET OFF THE BUS!

AND LAST BUT NOT LEAST, MY ALL-TIME FAVORITE . . .

. . . **KODOMO**, WHICH IS FOR LITTLE KIDS AND INCLUDES HUGE, WORLDWIDE HITS LIKE *CASE CLOSED* AND *DORAEMON*!

DORAEMON IS SO CUTE! ANYWAY, LET'S KEEP GOING . . . ! TIME FOR THE SUB-GENRES, WHICH DESCRIBE THE CONTENT OF THE STORIES . . .

DON'T TELL ME YOU KNOW ALL OF THEM . . . THERE ARE HUNDREDS!

OF COURSE I DON'T! THERE'S PRACTICALLY A SUB-GENRE FOR EVERYTHING!

SO . . . WHERE WOULD YOU PUT SLAM DUNK, FOR EXAMPLE?

AS WELL AS IN SHŌNEN?

YEAH.

THAT'S EASY: IT'S A **SPOKON** . . .

YOU SEE, YOU DO KNOW THINGS! AND TELL ME . . . WHAT DOES SPOKON MEAN?

UHHHH . . .

IT'S A COMBINATION OF THE WORD "SPORTS" . . .

. . . AND **KONJŌ** (WHICH MEANS "TENACITY", OR "PERSISTENCE.")

SPOKON STARTED TO DEVELOP AS A SUB-GENRE AROUND 1964 . . .

. . . WHEN JAPAN HOSTED THE OLYMPIC GAMES.

THEY'RE SPORTS STORIES, IN WHICH THE CHARACTERS ARE OFTEN REWARDED FOR THEIR COMMITMENT AND PERSEVERANCE.

HEY! WHAT ARE YOU DOING?

I'M FILMING YOU SO I CAN GO OVER THIS LATER!

SOOOOO EMBARRASSING! ANYWAY . . .

ISEKAI

STORIES SET IN PARALLEL UNIVERSES, OFTEN CONNECTED TO VIDEO GAMES.

I DON'T HAVE TO TELL YOU THAT *SWORD ART ONLINE* IS A PERFECT EXAMPLE.

BATTLE MANGA

THESE FOCUS ON ACTION-PACKED BATTLES BETWEEN LOTS OF DIFFERENT CHARACTERS, WHO OFTEN HAVE INCREDIBLE SUPERPOWERS. OBVIOUSLY, THIS IS THE SUB-GENRE FOR TITLES LIKE *MY HERO ACADEMIA* OR *ONE PUNCH MAN*.

ADVENTURE MANGA

STORIES IN WHICH THE MAIN CHARACTER GOES ON A JOURNEY,

EITHER TO EXPLORE THE WORLD . . .

OR BECAUSE THEY'RE SEARCHING FOR SOMETHING. THE MOST FAMOUS EXAMPLE MIGHT BE *ONE PIECE*.

GOURMET MANGA

LIKE *FOOD WARS*. THESE STORIES FOCUS ON FOOD AND COOKING,

WHICH ARE A STARTING POINT FOR HUMAN DRAMAS, SIMILAR TO THE WAY SPOKON USES SPORTS.

GAKUEN MANGA

STORIES SET IN SCHOOLS (GAKUEN MEANS "SCHOOL.") *BLUE PERIOD*, OR *A SILENT VOICE* ARE BOTH REALLY GOOD EXAMPLES.

AND SCHOOL IS OBVIOUSLY A GREAT SETTING TO EXPLORE YOUNG PEOPLE'S PROBLEMS.

SLICE OF LIFE

AS THE TITLE SUGGESTS, THESE SHOW REAL LIFE AS NATURALISTICALLY AS POSSIBLE.

IF YOU LIKE THE SOUND OF THEM, YOU COULD TRY *MY BROTHER'S HUSBAND*, A REALISTIC EXPLORATION OF THE EVERYDAY LIFE OF A GAY COUPLE.

▶ WHAT MAKES MANGA DIFFERENT FROM WESTERN COMICS?

THERE ARE SO MANY, MAN! WHAT GENRE IS YOUR FIRST MANGA GONNA BE?

HMMM, I'M NOT SURE BUT . . .

. . . I'D LIKE TO TELL THE STORY OF A JAPANESE HEROINE . . .

. . . A WOMAN WHO LIVED A LONG TIME AGO BUT IS STILL INSPIRING PEOPLE TODAY.

AND WHO IS THIS PERSON?

MAYBE I'LL TELL YOU ONE DAY . . .

MAN! YOU ARE SOOO ANNOYING!

BUT I DON'T KNOW IF I'D USE THE JAPANESE READING ORDER.

DID I HEAR THAT RIGHT? YOU WANT TO WRITE A MANGA?!

OF COURSE, MOM! WHY DO YOU THINK I WANT TO MEET FUMIO?!?

WELL, I'M VERY HAPPY ABOUT THAT.

BUT THE ORDER IN WHICH YOU READ THE PANELS ISN'T EVERYTHING . . .

?!?

FIRST OF ALL, MANGA ARE USUALLY IN BLACK AND WHITE—APART FROM, IN SOME CASES, A FEW PAGES TOWARDS THE BEGINNING.

BUT SOMETIMES THERE ARE THESE, LIKE, SHADOWS, RIGHT?

THOSE ARE WHAT WE CALL "SCREEN TONES."

OF COURSE, IT'S PARTIALLY TRUE TO SAY THAT MANGA ARE READ "BACKWARD"— BECAUSE THEY'RE READ FROM RIGHT TO LEFT, LIKE MOST JAPANESE WRITING . . .

. . . SO IT'S ONLY "BACKWARD" FOR WESTERNERS!

漫画家 志望

SO IF I DON'T WRITE IN JAPANESE, THEN I COULD WORK FROM LEFT TO RIGHT?

OF COURSE!

AND YOU COULD MAKE IT ALL IN COLOR TOO?

OF COURSE! BLACK AND WHITE IS A MORE CLASSIC STYLE, BUT LOTS OF MANGA ARE IN COLOR!

MOST MANGA ARE SERIALIZED . . . THEIR STORIES UNFOLD IN DIFFERENT EPISODES, OR CHAPTERS, WHICH ARE RELEASED ONE AT A TIME . . .

THOUGH LOTS OF MANGA TELL STANDALONE STORIES!

SO—WHAT MAKES A MANGA DIFFERENT FROM A WESTERN COMIC?

WELL, TO BE HONEST . . . NOTHING!

?!?

OR I COULD SAY . . . EVERYTHING!

THE TRUTH IS THAT, IN JAPAN, THE WORDS "MANGA" AND "KOMIKKU" (COMICS) ARE INTERCHANGEABLE!

LET ME TELL YOU A COUPLE OF STORIES . . .

BUT FIRST, LET'S HAVE A NICE CUP OF TEA.

2

LIFE AS A MANGAKA

Now that you know a little more, I bet you're more convinced than ever that you want manga in your life. Even as someone who writes about manga, I would love to spend every day coming up with new stories. Could that be the job for you, too? Why not! Let's find out what being a mangaka is all about.

PEOPLE IN JAPAN READ A LOT OF MANGA.

AND ALL OVER THE WORLD . . .

THAT IS TRUE. BUT IN JAPAN, NEW MANGA OFTEN START OUT IN MAGAZINES . . .

. . . WHERE THEY'RE SERIALIZED: PUBLISHED IN INSTALMENTS OR CHAPTERS.

YOU WORKED FOR ONE OF THOSE MAGAZINES WHEN YOU WERE YOUNG, RIGHT?

SHE WORKED FOR *SHŌNEN JUMP*! IT'S ONE OF THE MOST POPULAR MAGAZINES IN JAPAN!

YES. WELL, ACTUALLY I WORKED FOR A MANGAKA, NOT THE MAGAZINE EDITOR.

RIGHT. BUT WHAT'S THE DIFFERENCE?

THE MANGAKA IS THE ARTIST THAT CREATES THE STORY; THE EDITOR IS THE PERSON WHO RUNS THE MAGAZINE. THE EDITOR HAS A LOT OF POWER. THEY CAN EVEN CHANGE THE STORY IF THEY THINK IT MIGHT HELP SELL THE MAGAZINE.

HMM . . . BUT WHERE DOES THE STORY COME FROM?

THE MANGAKA MIGHT HAVE AN IDEA FOR A STORY AND PITCH IT TO THE EDITOR . . .

. . . OR THE EDITOR MIGHT ASK A MANGAKA TO WRITE SOMETHING SPECIFIC.

SO, THE MANGAKA AND THE EDITOR START WORKING VERY CLOSELY TO PLAN THE STORY. THE MANGAKA LOOKS AFTER ALL THE CREATIVE ASPECTS—FROM THE SCRIPT TO THE STYLING OF EACH PAGE—ALTHOUGH SOMETIMES THE TEXT AND THE DRAWINGS ARE DONE BY TWO DIFFERENT PEOPLE.

THE EDITOR SUPPORTS AND FOLLOWS THE MANGAKA'S WORK AND MANAGES THEIR RELATIONSHIP WITH THE PUBLISHER.

ULTIMATELY, IT'S THE PUBLISHER THAT HAS THE POWER TO DECIDE WHETHER A STORY WILL BE MADE OR NOT. ONCE THE PUBLISHER APPROVES A PROJECT, THEN THE MANGAKA CAN START WORK.

IN THE EARLY STAGES, THE FOCUS IS ON DEVELOPING THE CHARACTERS. THIS IS DONE THROUGH SKETCHES AND TESTS TO WORK OUT WHO THE CHARACTERS ARE AND HOW THEY THINK; WHAT THEY LOOK LIKE, HOW THEY DRESS, HOW THEY BEHAVE . . .

THEN YOU START WORK ON THE FIRST CHAPTER AND DO A STORYBOARD, WHICH IN INDUSTRY JARGON IS KNOWN AS A **NAME**.

THE NAME IS THE FIRST DRAFT OF A MANGA. THE DRAWINGS ARE JUST OUTLINES AND ANY SPEECH OR THOUGHT BUBBLES ARE PROVISIONAL. THE NAME HELPS YOU TO GET A SENSE OF THE DIMENSIONS OF THE PAGES AND WHETHER THE NARRATIVE IS WORKING.

IF THE NAME IS APPROVED FOR PUBLICATION, YOU START DRAWING THE ACTUAL MANGA. NORMALLY EVERYTHING IS DRAWN IN PENCIL FIRST, THEN GONE OVER WITH INK.

WORKING FOR A MANGAKA WAS THE MOST INCREDIBLE, AND THE MOST STRESSFUL THING I'VE EVER DONE!

TO DEAL WITH THE LARGE AMOUNTS OF WORK THEY HAVE, MANGAKA OFTEN HIRE TEAMS OF ASSISTANTS.

INITIALLY, ASSISTANTS PERFORM VERY SIMPLE TASKS, LIKE APPLYING SCREEN TONES OR BLACK BACKGROUNDS. IN TIME, THOUGH, AS THEY GET TO KNOW THE MANGAKA'S STYLE, THEY WILL START TO DRAW MORE DETAILED BACKGROUNDS AND LOCATIONS.

THIS ALLOWS THE MANGAKA TO FOCUS THEIR ATTENTION ON DRAWING THE CHARACTERS, ESPECIALLY CLOSE-UPS AND EXPRESSIONS.

SOME MANGAKA PREFER TO WORK ALONE SO AS TO MAINTAIN FULL CONTROL OVER THEIR ART, WORK AT THEIR OWN PACE, OR SATISFY A NEED FOR PERFECTION.

BUT IT'S NOT ALWAYS POSSIBLE TO TAKE THAT APPROACH. WORKING FOR A MAGAZINE OFTEN MEANS VERY SHORT TURNAROUND TIMES AND PUBLICATION DEADLINES. IN THE CASE OF WEEKLY PUBLICATIONS (WEEKLIES), IT WOULD BE IMPOSSIBLE TO DELIVER THE REQUIRED NUMBER OF PAGES WITHOUT THE HELP OF A TEAM!

THE FIRST MANGAKA TO USE ASSISTANTS WAS OSAMU TEZUKA, WHO FOUND HIMSELF HAVING TO MANAGE SO MANY STORIES AT ONCE THAT HE STARTED A FULL-BLOWN COMPANY: TEZUKA PRODUCTIONS.

LOTS OF MANGAKA LEARNED THEIR CRAFT BY BEING ASSISTANTS: TAKEHIKO INOUE (*SLAM DUNK, VAGABOND*) WAS AN ASSISTANT TO TSUKASA HŌJŌ (*CITY HUNTER, CAT'S EYE*); TSUTOMU NIHEI (*BLAME*) WORKED FOR TSUTOMU TAKAHASHI (*SKY HIGH*); WHILE MOYOCO ANNO (*HAPPY MANIA*) WAS AN ASSISTANT TO KYŌKO OKAZAKI (*HELTER SKELTER*).

▶ DEADLINES ARE CRUCIAL

WHY DID YOU SAY IT WAS STRESSFUL WORKING FOR A MANGAKA?

IT'S AN EXHAUSTING JOB, PARTICULARLY FOR ANYONE WHO WORKS FOR WEEKLIES LIKE *SHŌNEN JUMP*!

ON AVERAGE, A WEEKLY CHAPTER IS AROUND 19 PAGES. THAT MEANS THAT EVERY MONTH THERE ARE AROUND 80 PAGES TO WRITE, DRAW, AND INK!
ALSO, BEAR IN MIND THAT WHEN YOU'RE MAKING A MANGA YOU NEED TO CREATE YOUR STORYBOARD A BIT IN ADVANCE . . .

WHOA! I WOULDN'T WANNA WORK FOR A MAGAZINE!

PEOPLE WHO WORK FOR A WEEKLY TEND TO SPEND THE FIRST TWO DAYS ON THE NAME, AND THEN DO LONG, GRUELING DRAWING SESSIONS TO GET THEIR PAGES READY IN A FEW DAYS!
BY CONTRAST, WORKING FOR A MONTHLY MAGAZINE—WHICH NORMALLY PRODUCES CHAPTERS OF 30–45 PAGES—ALLOWS YOU TO WORK AT A SLOWER PACE.

DON'T WORRY, IT'S A LITTLE DIFFERENT OUTSIDE OF JAPAN! AND EVEN IN JAPAN, SOME ARTISTS ARE ABLE TO WORK AT A DIFFERENT, MORE RELAXED PACE.

BUT IT IS TRUE THAT LOTS OF MANGAKA HAVE STRESSFUL LIVES, AND HAVE TO BEAR A LOT OF EXPENSES TO PAY FOR THEIR STUDIO AND ASSISTANTS.

OF COURSE! I HADN'T THOUGHT ABOUT THE SALARY! BUT . . . DOES A MANGAKA MAKE A LOT OF MONEY?

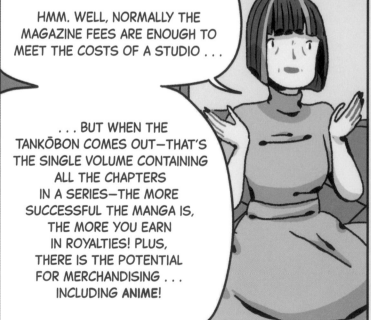

HMM. WELL, NORMALLY THE MAGAZINE FEES ARE ENOUGH TO MEET THE COSTS OF A STUDIO . . .

. . . BUT WHEN THE TANKŌBON COMES OUT—THAT'S THE SINGLE VOLUME CONTAINING ALL THE CHAPTERS IN A SERIES—THE MORE SUCCESSFUL THE MANGA IS, THE MORE YOU EARN IN ROYALTIES! PLUS, THERE IS THE POTENTIAL FOR MERCHANDISING . . . INCLUDING ANIME!

KOMAWARI IS A TERM REFERRING TO THE PRACTICE OF DIVIDING A PAGE INTO PANELS . . . AND IT REQUIRES A LOT OF SKILL!

IN JAPAN, PRE-FORMATTED DRAWING SHEETS ARE SOLD IN ART SHOPS. THESE **MANGA GENKŌ YŌSHI** (STANDARD MANGA SHEETS) ARE PRE-PRINTED WITH THE STANDARD DIMENSIONS USED FOR MANGA. THE INNER SECTION (IN YELLOW) INDICATES THE GRID USED FOR THE STORY PANELS.

IN SOME CASES, HOWEVER, DRAWINGS CAN EXTEND OUTSIDE THE YELLOW SECTION AND BLEED INTO THE RED ONE. THIS IS THE CASE WHEN YOU WANT TO CREATE PARTICULARLY DYNAMIC PAGES, OR EMPHASIZE SOME ASPECT OF THE SCENE. FOR THOSE WORKING DIGITALLY, THERE ARE TEMPLATES THAT REPRODUCE THE STANDARD MANGA SHEET.

AS FOR HOW MANY PANELS YOU USE, AND HOW YOU CHOOSE TO SPLIT THEM UP, MANGA WORKS ON A PRINCIPLE OF ABSOLUTE FREEDOM. IT'S THE TONE AND ACTION IN THE SCENE THAT DICTATE WHAT YOU DO! BUT IT IS OFTEN GOOD TO AVOID OVERCROWDING THE PAGES. DEPENDING ON THE FORMAT, A GOOD RULE OF THUMB IS TO STICK TO THREE OR FOUR HORIZONTAL ROWS, AND NOT EXCEED 8 PANELS PER PAGE.

THE MAIN FORMATS FOR MANGA ARE 5.3" X 6.8", 5.0" X 7.2", AND 5.8" X 8.2".

EVERY NOW AND THEN A FULL OR DOUBLE-PAGE DRAWING CAN HELP VARY THE PACE OF THE NARRATIVE.

SHŌNEN JUMP SUGGESTS AN AVERAGE OF 6 PANELS PER PAGE, AND 10 SPEECH OR THOUGHT BUBBLES.

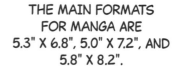

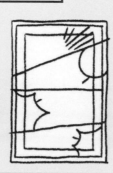

THE NAME HELPS TO ASSESS THE BALANCE OF SPACE AND CONTENT, TO CHECK IF THE NARRATIVE IS ENHANCED BY THE KOMAWARI CHOICES, AND ALSO TO WORK OUT THE AMOUNT OF TEXT ON A GIVEN PAGE.

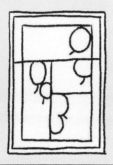
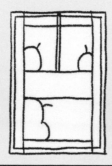

WHETHER YOU WORK IN ANALOG OR DIGITALLY, YOU STILL HAVE TO SCAN OR SAVE YOUR DRAWINGS IN A DIGITAL FORMAT SO THEY CAN BE INSERTED INTO THE PRINT LAYOUT WITH EDITING AND LAYOUT PROGRAMS LIKE INDESIGN.

. . . AND THESE ARE MY DIGITAL TOOLS . . .

RECOMMENDED RESOLUTIONS FOR DIGITAL FILES
• COLOR DRAWINGS: 450 DPI (DOTS PER INCH)
• BLACK-AND-WHITE DRAWINGS: 1200 DPI
• GRAYSCALE DRAWINGS (I.E. VARYING SHADES OF GRAY, RANGING FROM BLACK TO WHITE): 600 DPI
RECOMMENDED FORMATS IN WHICH TO SAVE DIGITAL FILES
• FOR PRINTING: AS A .TIFF FILE, COMPRESSED USING LZW
• FOR WEB AND VIDEO: AS A .JPG
IMAGE COLORS
• FOR COLOR PRINTING: CMYK (FOUR-COLOR)
• FOR WEB AND VIDEO: RGB (RED, GREEN, AND BLUE)

MOM, HOW DID IT WORK WHEN YOU WERE YOUNGER, WITHOUT ALL THIS TECHNOLOGY?

SO MANY THINGS WERE DIFFERENT WHEN I WAS YOUNGER . . .

TOKYO, 1998

IN THE STUDIO WHERE I WORKED, WE DREW EVERYTHING BY HAND . . .

. . . NOWADAYS THE TEXT IS INSERTED INTO THE DIGITAL FILES, BUT BACK THEN IT WAS CUT AND PASTED ONTO THE PAGES WITH GLUE.

THEN, WHEN THE PAGES WERE READY, THEY WERE HANDED TO A COURIER . . .

. . . OR THEY HAD TO BE DELIVERED TO THE EDITORIAL OFFICE IN PERSON. YOU CAN'T IMAGINE HOW MANY TIMES I FOUND MYSELF RUNNING ALL AROUND TOKYO . . .

THE "WEBTOON" IS A COLOR COMIC DESIGNED TO BE READ DIGITALLY, WITH PAGES ARRANGED VERTICALLY FOR THE READER TO SCROLL DOWN ON THEIR COMPUTER OR SMARTPHONE SCREEN. GIVEN THE OMNIPRESENCE OF THESE DEVICES, THE FORMAT HAS BECOME INCREASINGLY POPULAR. THERE ARE LOTS OF WEBTOON APPS: PICCOMA IS AMONG THE MOST FREQUENTLY USED IN JAPAN, BUT IT IS (UNFORTUNATELY) NOT AVAILABLE ABROAD. THE MOST COMMON IS WEBTOON, WHICH IS KOREAN BUT AVAILABLE ALL OVER THE WORLD. AND MORE APPS ARE COMING OUT ALL THE TIME.

> GETTING YOUR FOOT IN THE DOOR

THE INTERNET AND APPS HAVE MADE MANGA EVEN MORE ACCESSIBLE.

SO . . . DOES THAT MEAN IT'S EASIER TO GET PEOPLE TO READ YOUR STORIES?

I CAN'T BELIEVE THIS! WHEN WERE YOU GOING TO TELL ME . . .

. . . THAT YOU HAVE AN IDEA FOR A STORY TOO?!?!

HEY, YOU AIN'T THE ONLY ONE WITH AN IMAGINATION!

DO YOU KNOW WHAT MOCHIKOMI IS?

???

IT'S A PRACTICE THAT STILL EXISTS TODAY, WHEREBY AN ASPIRING MANGAKA CAN SUBMIT THEIR WORK TO AN EDITOR.

MANGA MAGAZINE WEBSITES NORMALLY HAVE A SPECIAL SECTION IN WHICH YOU CAN BOOK A MEETING OR SUBMIT YOUR WORK REMOTELY.

BUT THE SITES ARE ALL IN JAPANESE . . .

YES, BUT THERE ARE A FEW INITIATIVES AIMED AT THOSE WHO DON'T SPEAK JAPANESE . . .

OH YEAH? LIKE WHAT?

YOU CAN START BY LOOKING UP THESE ONES!

1. SILENT MANGA AUDITION
2. JAPAN INTERNATIONAL MANGA AWARD
3. MANGA PLUS CREATORS
4. CLIPSTUDIO

BACK IN MY DAY IT WOULD HAVE BEEN IMPOSSIBLE FOR JOHN TO WORK AS A MANGAKA IN JAPAN . . .

. . . OR EVEN PUBLISH A COMIC THERE.

HEY, THAT'S NOT FAIR!

I KNOW. BUT THINGS ARE CHANGING NOW.

BOICHI

BORN AND RAISED IN SOUTH KOREA, BOICHI IS NOW ONE OF THE LEADING MANGAKA AT SHUEISHA, THE PUBLISHING HOUSE BEHIND *SHŌNEN JUMP*.

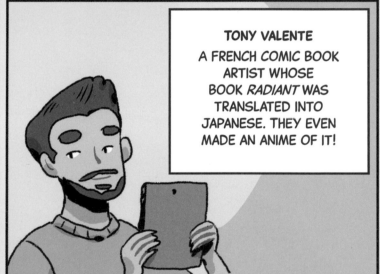

TONY VALENTE

A FRENCH *COMIC BOOK* ARTIST WHOSE BOOK *RADIANT* WAS TRANSLATED INTO JAPANESE. THEY EVEN MADE AN ANIME OF IT!

PEPPE

AN ITALIAN *COMIC BOOK* ARTIST WHO PUBLISHED A SERIES IN SHOGAKUKAN'S JAPANESE WEEKLY *BIG COMIC SPIRITS* CALLED *MINGO – DON'T GO THINKING ALL ITALIANS ARE A HIT WITH THE LADIES*, WHICH IS A COMEDY THAT LOOKS AT THE MISUNDERSTANDINGS AND STEREOTYPES SURROUNDING ITALIANS WHO LIVE IN JAPAN.

ÅSA EKSTRÖM

A SWEDISH *COMIC BOOK* ARTIST WHO STARTED PUBLISHING YONKOMA ON HER BLOG IN 2013, IN WHICH SHE RECORDED HER IMPRESSIONS OF JAPAN AS A WOMAN FROM NORTHERN EUROPE. THIS LED TO THE SERIES *NORDIC GIRL ÅSA DISCOVERS THE MYSTERIES OF JAPAN*.

3

BEFORE YOU START WRITING MANGA

Before you start working on your story, it's time to learn the technical, artistic, and narrative secrets of manga. "You never know when it might come in handy" as the old saying goes. And don't just read along; start practicing with pen and paper . . . or a tablet and mouse (or stylus)! Whether you're working in a digital or analog format, practice makes perfect!

LOTS OF MANGAKA SPENT YEARS DEVELOPING THEIR OWN UNIQUE STYLE!

WHEN HE WAS YOUNG, **EICHIRŌ ODA***, THE MANGAKA BEHIND *ONE PIECE*, USED TO PRACTICE BY COPYING THE STILLS OF DISNEY FILMS.

*EICHIRŌ ODA SOMETIMES DEPICTS HIMSELF WITH A FISH HEAD AS HIS TRADEMARK!

GO NAGAI—SUPER ROBOTS

GO NAGAI MADE HIS NAME IN JAPAN THANKS TO *HARENCHI GAKUEN* (SHAMELESS SCHOOL), BUT HE IS CREDITED FOR INVENTING THE **MECHA** GENRE. HIS *MAZINGER Z* IS THE FIRST MANGA TO FEATURE THE ICONIC SUPER ROBOTS CONTROLLED FROM INSIDE BY HUMAN PILOTS!

JUNJI ITO—THE KING OF HORROR

HORROR MANGA HAS A LONG HISTORY AND JUNJI ITO IS A MASTER OF THE FORM. HIS COSMIC THEMES, BODY HORROR, AND METICULOUSLY DRAWN LINES ARE IMMEDIATELY RECOGNIZABLE, PERHAPS MOST FULLY REALIZED IN THE TERRIFYING SPIRALS OF *UZUMAKI*, OR IN THE TITLE CHARACTER OF *TOMIE*, WITH HER BEWITCHING, SLANTING EYES, AND LONG, SILKY HAIR.

MOTO HAGIO—THE PRECURSOR TO BOYS' LOVE

THE HEART OF THOMAS IS COMMONLY THOUGHT OF AS THE FIRST **SHŌNEN AI** (BOYS' LOVE) STORY. PORTRAYING BEAUTIFUL TEENAGE PROTAGONISTS IN A EUROPEAN SETTING, IT LAID THE FOUNDATIONS FOR A NUMBER OF THE SUB-GENRE'S FEATURES.

AI YAZAWA—FASHION IN MANGA

FIRST WITH *PARADISE KISS*—AND LATER WITH *NANA*—YAZAWA DEPICTED THE LIVES OF YOUNG PEOPLE IN TOKYO'S VIBRANT UNDERGROUND SCENE. HER DISCERNING, DETAIL-ORIENTED EYE INCLUDED A RANGE OF REFERENCES TO STREET FASHION AND PUNK, PARTICULARLY VIVIENNE WESTWOOD.

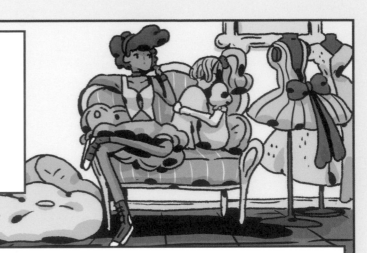

TAKEHIKO INOUE—REVIVING SPOKON

WHOLE GENERATIONS DEVELOPED A PASSION FOR BASKETBALL AFTER *SLAM DUNK*, AND YET SPOKON WAS IN DECLINE AS A GENRE BEFORE INOUE BREATHED NEW LIFE INTO IT, ADDING COMIC TOUCHES TO THE FORM AND TACKLING IMPORTANT SUBJECTS LIKE BULLYING. HIS RECOGNIZABLE CHARACTER DESIGNS FEATURE HUGE BODIES WITH SMALL HEADS.

YOSHIHIRO TATSUMI—THE BIRTH OF GEKIGA

THE TERM *GEKIGA* WAS COINED IN 1957 BY A COLLECTIVE OF CARTOONISTS LED BY TATSUMI. THESE STORIES TEND TO BE DARK IN MOOD; WITH IMAGERY EVOKING POST-WAR JAPAN, AND CHARACTERS WHO ARE SOCIAL OUTCASTS.

HAJIME ISAYAMA—ICONIC TITANS

THOUGH ISAYAMA'S STYLE IS FAR FROM CONVENTIONALLY BEAUTIFUL, THE SUCCESS OF *ATTACK ON TITAN* IS UNDENIABLE. INITIALLY DRAWN WITH ROUGH, STRAIGHTFORWARD LINES, THE STORY IS SET IN A WORLD THAT CANNOT READILY BE ASSOCIATED WITH A PARTICULAR CIVILIZATION OR TIME PERIOD, DOMINATED BY ICONIC, BARE-MUSCLED GIANTS. THE PIECE EVOLVED ENORMOUSLY OVER ITS 11 YEARS OF SERIALIZATION: ISAYAMA'S DRAWINGS BECAME MORE CONFIDENT, DEEPENING THE CHARACTERS' EXPRESSIVE QUALITIES.

CONVENTION DICTATES THAT A MANGA HAS THE FOLLOWING TECHNICAL FEATURES:

READING ORDER: TYPICALLY FROM RIGHT TO LEFT, BUT THIS ISN'T ESSENTIAL. A MANGA CREATED IN THE WEST CAN BE READ FROM LEFT TO RIGHT.

BLACK AND WHITE: MANGA ARE USUALLY PRINTED IN BLACK AND WHITE, BUT SOMETIMES ITS INITIAL PAGES—OR EVEN A WHOLE MANGA—CAN BE IN COLOR.

NUMBER OF PAGES: *TANKŌBON* ARE USUALLY ABOUT 200 PAGES LONG, BUT MANGA CAN BE LONGER OR SHORTER, PARTICULARLY IF THEY ARE STANDALONE STORIES.

FORMAT: THE FORMATS MENTIONED (SEE PAGE 27) ARE THE MOST COMMON, BUT THEY'RE NOT THE ONLY ONES USED IN MANGA.

BUT THERE ARE LOTS OF OTHER MORE SIGNIFICANT THINGS THAT DISTINGUISH MANGA.

EXAMPLE OF WESTERN GRAPHIC NOVEL

EXAMPLE OF JAPANESE MANGA

THROUGH THE KOMAWARI, MOST MANGAKA PAY CLOSE ATTENTION TO HOW THE PAGE IS SPLIT INTO PANELS. LEAF THROUGH ANY MANGA AND YOU'LL SEE UNEVEN, SLANTED PANELS, OR CHARACTERS BREAKING OUT OF THE FRAME. WESTERN COMICS TRADITIONALLY HAVE MORE STANDARDIZED LAYOUTS.

▶ VISUAL EFFECTS

ANOTHER ONE OF MANGA'S AESTHETIC FEATURES IS THE VISUAL EFFECTS CREATED BY HAND OR DIGITALLY DRAWN LINES.

SPEED LINES, ALSO KNOWN AS **MOTION LINES**, ARE USED TO CONVEY MOVEMENT. MOTION LINES ARE PARALLEL LINES (WITH OR WITHOUT SHADING) THAT CAN POINT IN DIFFERENT DIRECTIONS TO ACHIEVE DIFFERENT EFFECTS.

LINES FADING AWAY UPWARD

CONTINUOUS LINES

LINES FADING AWAY DOWNWARD

LATERAL LINES

FOCUS LINES DIRECT THE READER'S EYE TOWARD A PARTICULAR POINT. THE EFFECT CAN VARY DEPENDING ON THE THICKNESS OF THE LINES.

BETA FLASHES ACT LIKE THE NEGATIVE OF THE FOCUS LINES (I.E. WHITE ON A BLACK BACKGROUND). THEY ARE USED IN KEY SCENES, AND SIGNAL A SUDDEN REALIZATION.

THE STYLE OF THE SPEECH BUBBLE CONTRIBUTES TO THE MEANING OF THE WORDS IN IT.

OVAL-SHAPED.
USED FOR REGULAR SPEECH.
NORMALLY VERTICAL IN JAPAN AND HORIZONTAL IN THE WEST.

NEEDLE / BLAST.
USED WHEN THE WORDS ARE SPOKEN LOUDLY TO GIVE GREATER EMPHASIS TO WHAT IS BEING SAID.

CLOUD.
USED TO SUGGEST A SWEET TONE OF VOICE, OR SIGHING.

WAVY.
USED TO SUGGEST BREATHY, WEAK, OR FAINT SPEECH, OR TO CONVEY AGITATION, FEAR, WORRY, OR DOUBT.

RECTANGULAR.
USED FOR CAPTIONS, OR AS A SPACE FOR NARRATION, WHEN EITHER THE AUTHOR OR CHARACTERS ADDRESS THE READER DIRECTLY (FOR EXAMPLE, TO PROVIDE EXPOSITION.)

THOUGHT.
USED TO INDICATE THE INNER VOICE.

FLASH.
NORMALLY USED FOR UNSPOKEN LINES BETWEEN CHARACTERS (LIKE TELEPATHY), TO SUGGEST A SUDDEN AWARENESS OR "LIGHT BULB" MOMENT, OR THAT A HIGHER POWER IS ADDRESSING A CHARACTER WITHOUT SPEAKING OUT LOUD. THEY CAN EITHER BE BLACK ON A WHITE BACKGROUND, OR WHITE ON BLACK.

MULTISIDED, WITH ROUNDED EDGES.
USED TO COMMUNICATE A FLAT OR COLD TONE. IN JAPAN THEY OFTEN HAVE A DOUBLE BORDER, IN WHICH CASE THEY ARE USED FOR MECHANICAL VOICES OR THOSE COMING OUT OF RADIOS, TVS, AND TELEPHONES.

VISUAL EFFECTS

THE USE OF **SCREENTONES** SAVES THE MANGAKA A LOT OF TIME. SCREENTONES ARE CUT OR "SCRATCHED" OUT OF ADHESIVE SHEETS WITH A PAPER CUTTER. THIS DETAILED WORK TAKES SKILL AND A STEADY HAND!

GRADATION SCREENTONES, IN WHICH DOTS ARE DISTRIBUTED IN SUCH A WAY AS TO SHIFT FROM LIGHT TO DARK. THEY GIVE OBJECTS A SENSE OF DEPTH AND THREE-DIMENSIONALITY. THEY CAN ALSO BE USED ON CHARACTERS' HAIR AND FACES.

NET SCREENTONES ARE USED TO CREATE SHADOWS (FACES, FOLDS OF CLOTHES, BACKGROUNDS), AND COME IN VARYING DENSITIES.

EFFECT SCREENTONES REPRODUCE EFFECT LINES SUCH AS MOTION LINES OR OTHER ELEMENTS THAT CONVEY A CHARACTER'S MOOD. BY USING THESE, ARTISTS CAN AVOID HAVING TO COLOR IN THE WHOLE BACKGROUND.

PATTERN SCREENTONES RECREATE PATTERNS, SUCH AS FLOWERS, SQUARES, STARS, OR MUSICAL NOTES. THERE ARE MANY DIFFERENT TYPES WHICH CAN BE USED FOR PATTERNS ON CLOTHING, OBJECTS, OR BACKGROUNDS.

TODAY, IT IS POSSIBLE FOR MANGAKA TO APPLY SCREENTONES TO DRAWINGS DIGITALLY.

ONOMATOPOEIA ARE A VITAL PART OF THE PAGE; THEY'RE USED TO EXPRESS SOUNDS VISUALLY. AND BECAUSE THEY'RE HAND-DRAWN, ONOMATOPOEIA ALSO REVEAL A MANGAKA'S STYLE.

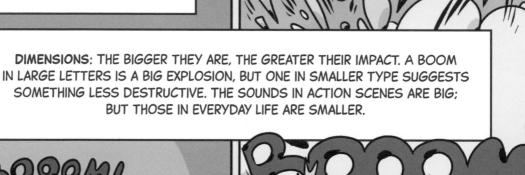

DIMENSIONS: THE BIGGER THEY ARE, THE GREATER THEIR IMPACT. A BOOM IN LARGE LETTERS IS A BIG EXPLOSION, BUT ONE IN SMALLER TYPE SUGGESTS SOMETHING LESS DESTRUCTIVE. THE SOUNDS IN ACTION SCENES ARE BIG; BUT THOSE IN EVERYDAY LIFE ARE SMALLER.

THICKNESS: SHARP NOISES ARE DRAWN WITH THINNER LINES, WHILE ANYTHING THAT INVOLVES IMPACT OR WEIGHT IS THICKER.

COLORS: THE SAME ONOMATOPOEIA, DRAWN ALL IN BLACK, OR IN WHITE WITH A BLACK BACKGROUND OR WITH A CROSS-HATCHED EFFECT, WOULD ACHIEVE A DIFFERENT RESULT. FOR EXAMPLE, BLACK SUGGESTS HEAVINESS, WHILE WHITE SUGGESTS LIGHTNESS.

SHAPE: THE SHAPES OF LETTERS ACHIEVE DIFFERENT EFFECTS. FOR EXAMPLE, SHARP-EDGED LETTERS SUGGEST HARDNESS; ROUNDED ONES SUGGEST SOFTNESS. A SUDDEN CRACK SHOULD BE DRAWN WITH SHARPER EDGES.

GENRE: IF THE STORY IS A HORROR OR A THRILLER, SPIKIER, JAGGED LETTERS ARE MORE SUITABLE. BUT IF IT'S A SHŌJO, TRY DRAWING SOFTER AND MORE ROUNDED LINES.

THERE ARE SO MANY THINGS TO LEARN!

HOW AM I GONNA REMEMBER ALL OF THAT?

DON'T WORRY ABOUT MEMORIZING IT RIGHT NOW.

THERE WILL BE PLENTY OF TIME TO PRACTICE!

IT SOUNDS TO ME LIKE YOU BOTH ALREADY HAVE A FEW IDEAS FOR YOUR MANGA . . .

I MEAN, YEAH, BUT . . .

WELL, I . . . SORT OF . . .

COME ON, DON'T KEEP ME WAITING!

HAVING AN IDEA IS REALLY IMPORTANT: THAT'S WHERE YOU START FROM TO DEVELOP YOUR SYNOPSIS.

THE SYNOPSIS IS A SHORT DOCUMENT SUMMARIZING THE STORY FROM START TO FINISH.

IT DESCRIBES THE CHARACTERS, PLACES, AND TIME PERIOD IN WHICH THE STORY IS SET AND THE IMPORTANT PLOT BEATS, SUCH AS THE BEGINNING, MID-POINT, AND ENDING!

THERE IS NO DIALOGUE IN A SYNOPSIS, BUT IT DESCRIBES HOW THE CHARACTERS INTERACT.

ONCE THE SYNOPSIS HAS BEEN WRITTEN, IT'S TIME TO DO SOME RESEARCH AND GATHER INFORMATION RELATING TO THE STORY. THESE MIGHT INCLUDE PHOTOS OR ILLUSTRATIONS OF THE SETTING—TO UNDERSTAND HOW TO DRAW THE PEOPLE IN IT, THEIR CLOTHES, OR THE INSIDES OF THEIR HOUSES, FOR EXAMPLE.

ONCE THE SYNOPSIS AND RESEARCH PHASES ARE DONE, IT'S TIME TO WRITE THE SCRIPT.

▶ WRITING YOUR SCRIPT

THE SCRIPT IS THE DOCUMENT WITH DESCRIPTIONS OF ALL THE SCENES, INCLUDING DETAILS OF TIME AND PLACE FOR EACH ONE.

IT ALSO INCLUDES ALL THE DIALOGUE AND THE MANGAKA'S DETAILED NOTES ON HOW THE SCENES SHOULD LOOK ON THE PAGE.

THE SCRIPT IS SPLIT INTO PAGES, WHICH ARE IN TURN SPLIT UP INTO PANELS.

Interior. Day.
The kitchen of an old house in the countryside near Tokyo. It's nearly lunchtime. It's spring. Trees and blue sky can be seen through the windows.

Panel 1
Girl (close-up; she's visibly angry because she's hungry): Moooooommmmm! Is it ready yet?

Panel 2
Wider shot: the child's mother, seen from behind, is making lunch. On the left, the girl, 5, pulls on her mom's blouse. The mom's head is turned towards her daughter; smiling at her.
Mom: Sweetie, you're so impatient! It'll be ready in five minutes.

Panel 3
Medium shot: The mom leans down towards the girl, who's still a bit annoyed; in a sweet voice, she says to her:
Mom: Have you washed your hands?
Girl: Why do I always have to wash my hands?

IF THE MANGAKA IS BOTH THE ILLUSTRATOR AND SCRIPTWRITER, THE SCRIPT CAN BE DONE AS A NAME—THE ROUGHLY SKETCHED-OUT STORYBOARD IN WHICH THE MANGAKA WORKS ON THE KOMAWARI, STRUCTURE, DIMENSIONS AND MEASUREMENTS OF THE ARTWORK, SPEECH BUBBLES, AND CAPTIONS.

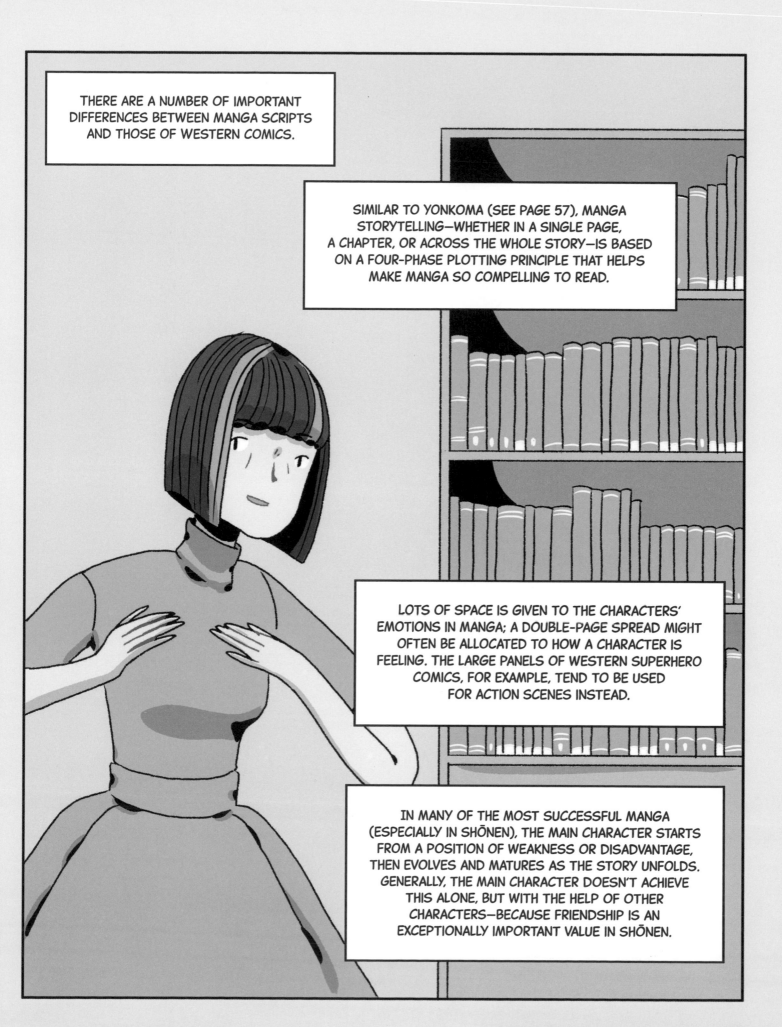

THERE ARE A NUMBER OF IMPORTANT DIFFERENCES BETWEEN MANGA SCRIPTS AND THOSE OF WESTERN COMICS.

SIMILAR TO YONKOMA (SEE PAGE 57), MANGA STORYTELLING—WHETHER IN A SINGLE PAGE, A CHAPTER, OR ACROSS THE WHOLE STORY—IS BASED ON A FOUR-PHASE PLOTTING PRINCIPLE THAT HELPS MAKE MANGA SO COMPELLING TO READ.

LOTS OF SPACE IS GIVEN TO THE CHARACTERS' EMOTIONS IN MANGA; A DOUBLE-PAGE SPREAD MIGHT OFTEN BE ALLOCATED TO HOW A CHARACTER IS FEELING. THE LARGE PANELS OF WESTERN SUPERHERO COMICS, FOR EXAMPLE, TEND TO BE USED FOR ACTION SCENES INSTEAD.

IN MANY OF THE MOST SUCCESSFUL MANGA (ESPECIALLY IN SHŌNEN), THE MAIN CHARACTER STARTS FROM A POSITION OF WEAKNESS OR DISADVANTAGE, THEN EVOLVES AND MATURES AS THE STORY UNFOLDS. GENERALLY, THE MAIN CHARACTER DOESN'T ACHIEVE THIS ALONE, BUT WITH THE HELP OF OTHER CHARACTERS—BECAUSE FRIENDSHIP IS AN EXCEPTIONALLY IMPORTANT VALUE IN SHŌNEN.

MANGA ALSO FEATURES A NUMBER OF RECURRING CHARACTER ARCHETYPES, PARTICULARLY IN THE LONG, SERIALIZED STORIES OF THE SHŌNEN AND SHŌJO GENRES.

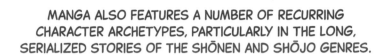

THE SHŌNEN HERO/INE

(LIKE IZUKU MIDORIYA, *MY HERO ACADEMIA*; YUKIHIRA SOMA, *FOOD WARS*) STRONG-MINDED AND GOOD-NATURED, THEY FACE THE CHALLENGES THAT COME THEIR WAY WITH GREAT DETERMINATION. THEY'RE OFTEN COMMITTED TO BEING THE BEST IN THEIR FIELD, WHETHER THAT'S SOMETHING FANTASTICAL OR MORE EVERYDAY, LIKE A SPORT, OR A PROFESSION.

MAHŌ SHŌJO (THE MAGICAL GIRL)

(LIKE SAKURA, *CARD CAPTOR SAKURA*) STORIES OF GIRLS WITH MAGICAL POWERS BECAME POPULAR IN THE 1960S. IN THE 1990S, THE MEETING OF MAGICAL POWERS AND THE ART OF COMBAT LED TO THE BIRTH OF *SAILOR MOON* AND ITS DERIVATIONS. THESE STORIES FEATURE YOUNG, FEMALE CHARACTERS WHO JUGGLE THE FIGHT AGAINST EVIL WITH THE DAY-TO-DAY PROBLEMS OF TEENAGE LIFE. IN 2011, THE ANIME BY GEN UROBUCHI, *PUELLA MAGI MADOKA MAGICA*, GAVE THE GENRE A HORROR TWIST.

THE BEST FRIEND

(LIKE KATSUYA JONOUCHI, *YU GI OH*; MIKASA ACKERMAN FROM *ATTACK ON TITAN*) IN MANGA, THE HERO CAN OFTEN ONLY ACHIEVE THEIR AIMS BECAUSE OF THE SUPPORT OF THEIR CLOSE FRIENDS. SOMETIMES THESE FRIENDS CAN BE COMPETITIVE OR JEALOUS, BUT THIS DRIVES THE MAIN CHARACTER TO DO EVEN BETTER. THE FEMALE CHARACTERS THAT FIT THIS ARCHETYPE PLAY INCREASINGLY IMPORTANT ROLES IN THEIR STORIES.

VILLAINS

(LIKE LIGHT YAGAMI, *DEATH NOTE*; DIO BRANDO, *JOJO'S BIZARRE ADVENTURE*) MANGA CAN HAVE ONE OVERALL VILLAIN, OR A RANGE OF BAD GUYS ACROSS DIFFERENT NARRATIVE ARCS. THEY CAN BE HEARTLESS AND CRUEL, CLEVER, AND CUNNING, AND ARE OFTEN THE MOST MEMORABLE CHARACTERS IN A STORY.

THE RIVAL

(LIKE GAROU, *ONE PUNCH MAN*; VEGETA, *DRAGONBALL Z*)
THESE AMBIVALENT CHARACTERS DON'T FIT THE ARCHETYPE OF A HERO OR A VILLAIN. THEY USUALLY CLASH WITH THE HERO BECAUSE THEY WANT TO BE STRONGER, OR BETTER AT SOMETHING, BUT END UP TEAMING UP WITH THEM AGAINST A BIGGER THREAT. RIVALS TEND TO BE MULTIFACETED CHARACTERS, AND IN SOME CASES A POPULAR VILLAIN BECOMES A RIVAL ONCE THE HERO HAS BEATEN THEM.

HETARE

(LIKE NOBITA, *DORAEMON*)
HETARE IS JAPANESE SLANG MEANING A COWARD; SOMEONE WEAK, GUTLESS, AND HESITANT. READERS ARE ENCOURAGED TO EMPATHIZE WITH THEIR JOURNEY AS THEY GROW TO BECOME BRAVER AND STRONGER.

BISHŌNEN

(LIKE SESSHOMARU, *INUYASHA*; GRIFFITH, *BERSERK*)
BISHŌNEN MEANS "BEAUTIFUL BOY." THESE ARE MALE CHARACTERS WHO HAVE A STRIKING, ANDROGYNOUS BEAUTY. BOTH HEROES AND VILLAINS CAN BE BISHŌNEN, BUT MORE OFTEN THAN NOT IT IS THE RIVAL WHO HAS THIS FEATURE.

BISHŌJO

(LIKE ORIHIME INOUE, *BLEACH*; ELIZABETH, *SEVEN DEADLY SINS*)
BISHŌJO MEANS "BEAUTIFUL GIRL." FEMALE CHARACTERS PORTRAYED WITH FEMININE AND KAWAII (CUTE) FEATURES. THE CHILDHOOD FRIEND IS OFTEN DEPICTED AS A BISHŌJO.

BUT TO BUILD YOUR CHARACTERS YOU HAVE TO WORK ON THEM ON MORE THAN JUST A VISUAL LEVEL . . .

YOU HAVE TO THINK ABOUT HOW THEY BEHAVE AND WORK THAT INTO YOUR DRAWINGS.

TRY DRAWING YOURSELVES. IT'S A GOOD EXERCISE.

SIT DOWN HERE, NEXT TO ME, AND I'LL SHOW YOU HOW TO START.

JOHN, I'LL HAVE TO ASK YOU A FEW QUESTIONS THOUGH . . .

YOKO
- 17 YEARS OLD
- ONLY CHILD
- GREW UP IN A CREATIVE ENVIRONMENT
- LIKES DRAWING
- LIKES READING MANGA
- A BIT OF A DREAMER.
- GENEROUS, EMOTIONAL, JEALOUS . . .
- AND A LITTLE COMPETITIVE!

JOHN
- 16 AND A HALF (BUT ALREADY TELLS PEOPLE HE'S 17)
- THE YOUNGEST CHILD OF THREE
- HIS FAMILY IS ALL SPORTY; HE ISN'T SO MUCH.
- LIKES ACTION, BUT IS KIND OF LAZY!
- LIKES DRAWING
- LIKES READING MANGA
- ENTHUSIASTIC, CURIOUS, HONEST, BOLD . . .
- AND A LITTLE COMPETITIVE!

WOW! I FEEL LIKE WE COULD BE MANGA CHARACTERS!

SO COOL!

COME ON, JOHN, LET'S GO SEE FUMIO!

4

GETTING STARTED BY FUMIO OBATA

It's not every day that you have a real mangaka all to yourself, teaching a class on how to make manga. Yoko and John are lucky enough to have that chance . . . and so do you! Don't miss this key lesson from internationally renowned manga artist **Fumio Obata**. With his guidance, you'll be able to get started and bring your story to life. Don't forget your drawing and writing tools!

PART 1: START SIMPLE

HELLO GUYS

HI FUMIO!

HAVE YOU LEARNED A LOT ABOUT MANGA SO FAR?

HI YOKO. HI JOHN, REALLY GOOD TO SEE YOU. WELCOME TO MY STUDIO.

AND WELCOME TO MY MANGA CLASS!

YOU MAY ALREADY HAVE SOME IDEAS AND CHARACTERS THAT YOU CAN'T WAIT TO TURN INTO MANGA.

YES!

I CAN'T WAIT.

HOLD ON!

THERE'S A LOT TO LEARN, SO LET'S START WITH THE BASICS.

MAKING MANGA IS LIKE RUNNING A MARATHON.

IT'S BEST TO START WITH SHORT RUNS. THEN YOU GRADUALLY BUILD UP TO LONGER AND LONGER DISTANCES.

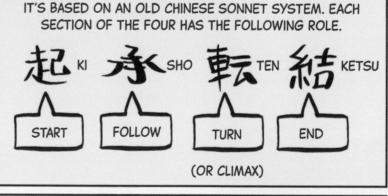

HERE IS A YONKOMA EXAMPLE WITH A CLEAR EMPHASIS ON 'TEN'!

起
START

I CAN'T TELL YOU ENOUGH HOW IMPORTANT THE STORY IS IN MANGA.

TO KEEP YOURS FROM FEELING FLAT AND PREDICTABLE, STUDYING "TEN" IS SO IMPORTANT.

承
FOLLOW

WHY IS MANGA SO GOOD? BECAUSE IT IS FULL OF GREAT TWISTS BUT IS ALSO RELATABLE.

YONKOMA IS WHERE YOU CAN START LEARNING THESE SPIRITS AND ESSENCES.

転
TURN

PIPIPI

結
END

PHEW!

LET'S LOOK AROUND AND FIND A RELATABLE MOTIF. THEN MAKE A YONKOMA MANGA USING KI-SHO-TEN-KETSU!

I WILL SHOW YOU ANOTHER EXAMPLE.

THE OTHER DAY I BROKE THIS VASE BY ACCIDENT WHILE CLEANING MY ROOM.

AND I WOULD LIKE A PHONE TO PLAY A KEY ROLE IN THIS YONKOMA.

➤ **FROM YONKOMA TO KOMAWARI**

YONKOMA TO KOMAWARI

LET'S EXPLORE HOW YONKOMA MANGA ARE ADAPTED TO THE CLASSIC KOMAWARI LAYOUT.

ONE: PREPARE YONKOMA

Meow

MEEO? OOW!!

GOSH, WHAT A WEIRD DREAM.

AH, IT WAS BECAUSE OF YOU, WASN'T IT?

?

TWO: TRANSFER

NOW THINK OF IT IN TERMS OF PAGES. I RECOMMEND TWO PAGES FOR ADAPTING ONE YONKOMA.

PAGE 1 PAGE 2

PLAN 5-6 PANELS PER PAGE AND SLOT IN YOUR YONKOMA PANELS WHERE APPROPRIATE.

Meow

THREE: ADD NEW SCENES

CURR!

Meow

MEEO OOW!!

THINK OF THESE NEW ADDITIONS AS "BUILD-UPS" BETWEEN THE ORIGINAL YONKOMA PANELS.

EXERCISE TIME

MAKE UP A COMEDIC STORY AND TURN IT INTO A YONKOMA. INVENT A TWIST OR CLIMAX MOMENT AT THE THIRD OR FOURTH PANEL.

THEN YOU CAN TRY TO ADAPT IT TO CLASSIC MANGA KOMAWARI, LIKE I HAVE JUST DONE.

GETTING STARTED   61

CREATING CHARACTERS: START FROM THE BASICS

HOW ABOUT TURNING YOURSELF INTO A CHARACTER?

OH, YEAH!

UNCLE GEORGE?

OR SOMEONE YOU KNOW VERY WELL.

YOU CAN GROW YOUR CHARACTER BY CREATING MORE SHORT EPISODES WITH THE YONKOMA METHOD.

KNOWING A FEW TRAITS IS ENOUGH TO GET STARTED AND MAKE A SERIES.

IT'S A PROCESS OF DISCOVERING YOUR CHARACTER. THEY'RE WAITING FOR YOUR DIRECTION.

LET'S SEE HOW YOKO'S YONKOMA CHARACTER EVOLVES!

IF THE CHARACTER HAS A SUPERNATURAL POWER, MAYBE MAKE A YONKOMA ABOUT THAT.

I CAN MAKE PLANTS AND TREES TALK!

THEN MAYBE ONE OR TWO YONKOMA ON THEIR APPEARANCE, OR ANY PROPS THEY USE.

YOU MAY COME UP WITH A SIDEKICK AND ADD BACKGROUND CHARACTERS TO EXPAND THE WORLD OF THIS MANGA.

REMEMBER TO USE SHORT FORMATS FIRST. LET THE STORY GROW RATHER THAN WRITING A LONG PLAN.

ACTION SPEAKS MORE.

YOU CAN ALSO GIVE AN INTERESTING PAST TO YOUR CHARACTER.

CHARACTERS WITH PAST

DECIDE WHAT HAPPENED TO THEM BEFORE THE MANGA BEGINS.

WHirrr...

A POPULAR SETUP NOWADAYS WITH SHŌNEN MANGA CHARACTERS...

...IS THAT SOMETHING HAPPENED TO THEM THAT STARTED THEIR ADVENTURE.

WHirrrrr

THE PAST AFFECTS THEIR PRESENT. THEY MAY STRIVE FOR SURVIVAL OR REDEMPTION.

WE WONDER...

WHAT HAPPENED TO THEIR FAMILY?

WHAT DOES THAT TATTOO MEAN?

WHY CAN THEY SPEAK TO THE DEAD?

WHILE WE, THE READERS, CAN ONLY GUESS WHAT HAPPENED BEFORE IT IS REVEALED, WE STILL BECOME ATTACHED TO THE CHARACTER AS WE TRAVEL WITH THEM.

THE MANGAKA DOES NOT GIVE OUT ALL THE ANSWERS AT ONCE. THAT'S WHAT MAKES US TURN THE PAGE.

HEARING THESE, YOU MAY ALREADY PICTURE SOME SCENES IN YOUR HEADS.

OH YES!

WHY NOT DRAW THOSE SCENES?

DEVELOPING YOUR ART STYLE

PART 3: YOUR MANGA STYLE

LASTLY, LET'S TALK ABOUT HOW TO DEVELOP YOUR OWN MANGA STYLE.

YOU MAY WELL BE AMBITIOUS WITH A STORY AND CHARACTERS THAT YOU WANT TO TURN INTO YOUR OWN MANGA SERIES.

BUT HOW MUCH DO THEY REPRESENT YOU AS A PERSON?

ARE YOUR IDEAS A BIT TOO SIMILAR TO YOUR FAVORITE MANGA OR ANIME?

MY MANGA STYLE?

NEVER THOUGHT OF THAT.

WHAT HAS MADE MANGA SO POPULAR IS THAT THESE FAMOUS AUTHORS EXPRESSED THEMSELVES IN THEIR STORIES AND CHARACTERS.

YES, THERE IS CERTAIN DEGREE OF CRAFTSMANSHIP TO MAKE IT ENTERTAINING,

BUT ULTIMATELY STORYTELLING IS ABOUT SELF-EXPRESSION.

STYLE
SELF-EXPRESSION

PAT PAT

IT'S ABOUT YOU!

HOW DO WE ALLOW THIS TO HAPPEN IN YOUR MANGA?

I WOULD SAY, PRACTICE BY DRAWING STORIES BASED ON YOUR LIFE EXPERIENCES.

YOUR FEELINGS AND OBSERVATIONS ARE GREAT SOURCES FOR STORYTELLING.

THIS SOUNDS LIKE "SLICE OF LIFE" GENRE, BUT THE IDEA RELATES TO EVERY MANGA CREATOR.

LET'S TRY IT.

FIRST, MAKE A SHORT SYNOPSIS.

WRITE ABOUT A MEMORABLE EXPERIENCE THAT YOU'VE HAD.

MEMORABLE EXPERIENCE?

YES

SYNOPSIS AND <u>REASON</u>

AND AT THE END OF THE SYNOPSIS, ADD A REASON WHY THAT MEMORY STUCK WITH YOU.

THIS WILL BE LIKE THE MESSAGE YOU WANT TO LEAVE YOUR READERS WITH.

MAKE SURE YOU KEEP THE SYNOPSIS SHORT AND CONCISE.

GO ON! WRITE!

HMMM...

10 MINUTES LATER

I HAVE DONE MINE, IT'S CALLED "STARS."

COULD YOU READ IT TO US?

OK.

IT WAS 10 YEARS AGO WHEN I WENT CAMPING WITH MY FAMILY FOR THE FIRST TIME.

IT WAS AMAZING TO SEE ALL THE NATURE.

▶ DRAW FROM YOUR EXPERIENCE

I LOVED SEEING THE WATERFALL SO CLOSE-UP.

THE NOISE WAS LIKE NOTHING I'D EVER HEARD!

I SAW THE BEAUTIFUL COLORS IN THE TREES,

AND HEARD HOW SWEET THE BIRDSONG WAS. IT SOUNDED SO FRIENDLY.

BUT THE MOST MEMORABLE MOMENT WAS . . .

WOW!

SEEING THE NIGHT SKY FILLED WITH BRIGHT STARS.

I THOUGHT ABOUT JUST HOW BIG THE UNIVERSE WAS . . .

. . . AND HOW SMALL I MUST HAVE LOOKED, IF SOMEONE WAS WATCHING FROM THE STARS!

IS IT OK? I'M NOT SURE IF I'M DOING IT RIGHT.

ABSOLUTELY, IT'S A NICE MESSAGE!

JOHN, HAVE YOU GOT YOURS?

WELL, KIND OF . . .

IT'S CALLED "OUTAGE."

IN ONE SUMMER, THERE WAS A THUNDER STORM IN THE MIDDLE OF NIGHT . . .

. . . CAUSING A MASSIVE OUTAGE IN OUR AREA.

WE ATE UNDER CANDLELIGHT.

THE NEXT DAY WE CHECKED THE DAMAGE IN OUR NEIGHBORHOOD

AND SPOKE TO SOME NEIGHBORS FOR THE FIRST TIME IN YEARS.

WE DID SOME CLEAN-UP JOBS TOGETHER.

THE POWER WAS STILL OUT, SO SOME PEOPLE BROUGHT OUT EMERGENCY BATTERY UNITS FOR OTHERS.

THERE WAS A NICE VIBE, DESPITE THE INCONVENIENCE.

THEN I READ NEW YORK HAD A MASSIVE BLACKOUT IN 2003.

AND PEOPLE WENT THROUGH SIMILAR BONDING MOMENTS.

SORRY, BUT I COULDN'T THINK OF ANY MESSAGE FOR IT.

DON'T WORRY. I THINK THERE'S SOMETHING THERE.

> EVERYONE HAS THEIR OWN STORY

EXERCISE TIME

JUST LIKE HOW I VISUALIZED EACH LINE OF YOKO AND JOHN'S SYNOPSIS, ILLUSTRATE YOUR OWN EXPERIENCE THAT HAPPENED IN REAL LIFE.

IT CAN BE TRIVIAL STUFF BUT SHOULDN'T BE A SIMPLE DESCRIPTION OF AN EVENT.

IT TOUCHED ME BECAUSE—

I FELT GRATEFUL BECAUSE—

BE HONEST WITH HOW YOU FELT, LIKE SENDING A MESSAGE TO A FRIEND.

IF YOU PREFER, YOU CAN MIX IN SOME FICTION, OR USE A FICTIONAL CHARACTER YOU CREATE.

YOUR STORY CAN BE EXTENDED INTO A LENGTHIER NARRATIVE, LIKE HOW YONKOMAS CAN BE REFORMATTED.

YOUR PERSONAL EXPERIENCES BRING REALITY INTO YOUR STORYTELLING.

SO WHY NOT TO INCORPORATE THEM INTO YOUR MAIN MANGA PLAN TOO?

IT COULD BE USED IN A FLASHBACK SCENE OR A SUB-PLOT.

IN MANGA, CHARACTERS HAVE MOMENTS TO REFLECT ON THEIR ACTIONS. THESE OFTEN COME FROM THE AUTHORS' REAL-LIFE EXPERIENCES, AND IT HELPS THE READER RELATE TO THEM.

EXPERIENCE

AUTHOR

MY ACTION

DIARY

BE RECEPTIVE TO YOUR OWN LIFE STORY BECAUSE THAT'S WHAT MAKES YOUR VOICE UNIQUE!

6 RECOMMENDED ACTIVITIES FOR MAKING ORIGINAL MANGA.

START WITH SHORT STORIES. IF YOU ARE STUCK, USE YOUR OWN EXPERIENCE, OR ADAPT A STORY YOU KNOW.

2 PAGES? 4 PAGES? 8 PAGES?

EXPLORE THINGS OUTSIDE YOUR USUAL INTERESTS.

THINK OF A THEME OR MESSAGE THAT YOU WANT TO DELIVER.

WHAT IS THAT I WANT TO TALK ABOUT?

READ BOOKS, WATCH FILMS, AND STAY IN TUNE WITH CURRENT AFFAIRS.

DVD

NEWS

AMAZON NETFLIX

CARRY SKETCHBOOKS AND REGULARLY DRAW AND WRITE.

DON'T MOVE!

?

VISIT EXHIBITIONS AND GALLERIES.

LASTLY, AT THE CORE OF EVERY GOOD MANGA THERE IS A GOOD STORY. TO WRITE IT, DISCOVER MORE ABOUT THE WORLD AND BUILD EXPERIENCES AS A PERSON. IT'S PERFECTLY FINE TO ENJOY WITH OTHER ACTIVITIES . . . SPORTS, MUSIC, TRAVELING, OR FASHION, TO NAME A FEW!

I LOVE PLAYING GUITAR. MUSIC TAUGHT ME A LOT ABOUT STORYTELLING.

WE HOPE YOU ENJOY THE EXERCISES.

GOOD LUCK ON YOUR MANGA JOURNEY!

5

MANGA ICONS

Your dreams are the same as those of every mangaka before you. Today's greats began by reading the work of the great mangaka that came before them; they learned their stories by heart, studied their characters, and even practiced by redrawing them. Over the next few pages I'll introduce you to some mangaka who are worth getting to know.

OSAMU TEZUKA

1928–1989

AS A BOY, TEZUKA WAS KNOWN FOR HIS RICH IMAGINATION, AND HIS REMARKABLE PASSION FOR INSECTS! GROWING UP IN A LIBERAL ENVIRONMENT, HE READ COMICS AND WATCHED DISNEY FILMS, BOTH OF WHICH WOULD HAVE AN INFLUENCE ON HIS REVOLUTIONARY STYLE. IT IS TO HIM THAT WE OWE THE EMERGENCE OF "STORY MANGA" (I.E. MANGA WITH LONGER, MORE INTRICATE PLOTS, AS OPPOSED TO THE SHORTER, MORE EPISODIC COMICS THAT WERE POPULAR IN JAPAN BEFORE THE SECOND WORLD WAR), WHICH IS WHY TODAY HE IS REMEMBERED AS THE "GOD OF MANGA."

BUT HIS INFLUENCE ON THE JAPANESE POPULAR IMAGINATION DOESN'T STOP AT MANGA. IN 1961, AFTER WORKING AT TOEI ANIMATION, TEZUKA FOUNDED HIS OWN ANIMATION STUDIO, MUSHI PRODUCTION—AND LATER TEZUKA PRODUCTIONS—WHICH LAID THE FOUNDATIONS FOR THE MODERN ANIME INDUSTRY. HIS ANIME SERIES *ASTRO BOY* WAS THE FIRST OF ITS KIND TO BE BROADCAST OUTSIDE OF JAPAN, WHILE *KIMBA THE WHITE LION* WAS THE FIRST ANIME TO BE MADE IN COLOR.

FUN FACT

TEZUKA HAD A DEGREE IN MEDICINE, AN EXPERIENCE THAT MEANT THAT HE COULD ADD LOTS OF RICH, SPECIFIC DETAILS TO *BLACK JACK*, A MANGA ABOUT THE ADVENTURES OF AN UNLICENSED SURGEON.

RIYOKO IKEDA

1947

IKEDA GREW UP AS A LOVER OF THE GREAT CLASSICS OF LITERATURE, THANKS TO HER FAMILY'S WELL-STOCKED BOOKSHELVES. SHE DISCOVERED COMIC BOOKS (AND TEZUKA'S WORK IN PARTICULAR) AT A FRIEND'S HOUSE, FAR FROM THE SEVERE, DISAPPROVING EYES OF HER PARENTS, WHO FORBID HER FROM BUYING MANGA. SHE WAS IMMEDIATELY HOOKED!

DETERMINED TO COMBINE HER PASSION FOR HISTORICAL FICTION WITH COMICS, IN 1972 SHE SUBMITTED A PROPOSAL TO THE EDITORS OF *MARGARET* MAGAZINE FOR A SERIES SHE WOULD WRITE AND ILLUSTRATE. SET DURING THE FRENCH REVOLUTION, IT WAS ENTITLED *THE ROSE OF VERSAILLES* AND WOULD TELL THE STORY OF LADY OSCAR, A COMMANDER OF THE ROYAL GUARD AT THE COURT OF MARIE ANTOINETTE. THE PUBLISHERS WERE SKEPTICAL ABOUT THE IDEA OF A HISTORICAL, FEMALE-LED MANGA, BUT CONSENTED TO PUBLICATION ON THE CONDITION THAT THEY COULD WITHDRAW IT IMMEDIATELY IF IT WASN'T SUCCESSFUL. NEEDLESS TO SAY, IT WAS AN ABSOLUTE HIT! IKEDA IS NOW CONSIDERED ONE OF THE MOST IMPORTANT MANGAKA OF THE "YEAR 24 GROUP:" A GROUP OF FEMALE MANGA ARTISTS WHO REVOLUTIONIZED THE SHŌJO GENRE BY INTRODUCING MORE DRAMATIC ELEMENTS, AS WELL AS GIVING ITS CHARACTERS GREATER PSYCHOLOGICAL DEPTH AND COMPLEXITY.

FUN FACT

IKEDA IS ALSO A SINGER. SHE HAS A SOPRANO VOCAL RANGE AND HAS RELEASED RECORDS AND PERFORMED LIVE. HER PASSION FOR OPERA HAS ALSO HAD AN INFLUENCE ON HER WORK: IN 2000 SHE ADAPTED WAGNER'S *THE RING OF THE NIBELUNG* CYCLE INTO A MANGA.

AKIRA TORIYAMA
1955-2024

BORN INTO A POOR FAMILY, TORIYAMA WAS PASSIONATE ABOUT DRAWING FROM AN EARLY AGE. HIS HEROES WERE OSAMU TEZUKA AND WALT DISNEY, AND HE PARTICULARLY LOVED *ONE HUNDRED AND ONE DALMATIANS*. HE MADE HIS DEBUT AS A MANGAKA IN 1978, AFTER STUMBLING ON A COMPETITION RUN BY *SHŌNEN JUMP*, AND STARTED PUBLISHING A FEW SHORT STORIES. BUT HIS FIRST REAL SUCCESS CAME IN 1980 WITH THE *DR. SLUMP* SERIES.

THANKS TO HIS UNIQUE BRAND OF WACKY HUMOR, TORIYAMA QUICKLY ACQUIRED A HUGE READERSHIP. IN 1984, ONLY A FEW MONTHS AFTER FINISHING *DR. SLUMP*, HE BEGAN WRITING A BATTLE MANGA THAT WOULD MARK THE CHILDHOODS OF GENERATIONS OF READERS: *DRAGON BALL*. INSPIRED BY THE SIXTEENTH-CENTURY CHINESE NOVEL *JOURNEY TO THE WEST*, *DRAGON BALL* CHRONICLES THE ADVENTURES OF SON GOKU AND HIS FRIENDS AS THEY SEARCH FOR THE SEVEN DRAGON BALLS—MAGICAL CRYSTAL SPHERES THAT CAN GRANT ANY WISH. TO THIS DAY *DRAGON BALL* REMAINS ONE OF THE MOST POPULAR AND BESTSELLING MANGA IN HISTORY.

FUN FACT
TORIYAMA REPORTEDLY WATCHED A LOT OF JACKIE CHAN KUNG-FU MOVIES AS HE WAS DRAWING *DRAGONBALL*—WHICH MUST HAVE BEEN A MAJOR SOURCE OF INSPIRATION FOR THE MARTIAL ARTS FEATURED IN THE STORY!

KENTARO MIURA

1966–2021

MIURA DREW HIS FIRST COMICS IN ELEMENTARY SCHOOL, AND AS HIS WORK DEVELOPED, HE WAS INFLUENCED BY GO NAGAI AND TETSUO HARA (*FIST OF THE NORTH STAR*) AS WELL AS THE *STAR WARS* FILMS. HE MADE HIS MAGAZINE DEBUT IN 1985, WHEN HE SENT TWO STORIES TO *WEEKLY SHŌNEN* MAGAZINE. ONE OF THE TWO, *FUTATABI*, WAS AWARDED A PRIZE AND PUBLISHED.

HOWEVER, AFTER THAT FIRST PUBLICATION, MIURA WENT THROUGH A TOUGH PERIOD IN WHICH ALL OF HIS PROPOSALS WERE REJECTED. THIS CRISIS CAME TO AN END IN 1988 WHEN HE MANAGED TO GET A STANDALONE STORY PUBLISHED IN *COMICOMI* MAGAZINE. THE STORY FOLLOWED THE EXPLOITS OF GUTS, A LONE WARRIOR, AND SERVED AS THE PROTOTYPE FOR *BERSERK*, HIS MASTERPIECE, WHICH WOULD BE SERIALIZED STARTING THE FOLLOWING YEAR. WITH ITS COMPLEX NARRATIVE THAT UNFOLDS OVER MORE THAN 40 VOLUMES WRITTEN OVER 30 YEARS, *BERSERK* IS A DARK, VIOLENT FANTASY MANGA THAT TACKLES SUBJECTS AS VARIED AS FREE WILL, HUMAN RESILIENCE, BETRAYAL, AND REVENGE.

FUN FACT

AT THE AGE OF 18, MIURA WORKED AS AN ASSISTANT TO GEORGE MORIKAWA, THE CREATOR OF *HAJIME NO IPPO*. MORIKAWA THOUGHT MIURA WAS WASTING HIS TALENT WORKING AS AN ASSISTANT, SO HE FIRED HIM!

NAOKO TAKEUCHI

1967

TAKEUCHI BEGAN DRAWING MANGA IN HER LATE TEENS. WHEN SHE WAS 19, SHE WON A COMPETITION FOR EMERGING MANGA ARTISTS RUN BY KODANSHA, THE SAME PUBLISHER THAT WOULD EVENTUALLY PUBLISH HER BIGGEST HIT, *SAILOR MOON*. SERIALIZED FROM 1992 TO 1997 IN THE SHŌJO MAGAZINE *NAKAYOSHI*, SAILOR MOON IS ONE OF THE MOST ICONIC MANGA OF THE 1990S, AND ITS CHARACTERS STILL ENJOY AN ALMOST UNRIVALED POPULARITY TODAY.

THE STORY'S MAGICAL ELEMENTS—WHICH HAD ALREADY PROVED SUCCESSFUL FOR MANY **MAJOKKO** HEROINES—AS WELL AS ITS THEMES OF ADVERSITY (TRADITIONALLY MORE CONNECTED TO THE SHŌNEN GENRE), FRIENDSHIP, AND SISTERHOOD REFLECTED THE INCREASING FEMALE EMPOWERMENT AND EMANCIPATION IN JAPANESE SOCIETY AT THE TIME. *SAILOR MOON* IS ALSO A PERFECT EXAMPLE OF SUCCESS ACROSS DIFFERENT MEDIA, TAKING A VARIETY OF SHAPES AND FORMS: ANIMATED TV SERIES AND FEATURE FILMS, LIVE ACTION **TOKUSATSU**, MERCHANDISING, TOYS, AND MUSICALS, AS WELL AS NUMEROUS PARTNERSHIPS WITH FASHION AND MAKE-UP BRANDS.

FUN FACT

TAKEUCHI HAS A DEGREE IN CHEMISTRY AND NAMED MANY SAILOR MOON CHARACTERS AFTER MINERALS AND GEMSTONES.

MOYOKO ANNO
1971

ANNO IS THE NIECE OF FAMOUS MANGA ARTIST KO KOJIMA, AND EVEN AS A CHILD SHE LOVED DRAWING, WATCHING ANIME, AND READING MANGA. IN HER LAST FEW YEARS OF ELEMENTARY SCHOOL, AND LATER IN MIDDLE SCHOOL, ANNO WAS PART OF A MANGA CLUB WHERE SHE AND HER CLASSMATES CREATED *DŌJINSHI*, SELF-PRODUCED FAN FICTION MAGAZINES BASED ON THE MOST POPULAR MANGA OF THE TIME, SUCH AS *CAPTAIN TSUBASA*, AND *SAINT SEIYA*.

IN 1995 SHE STARTED PUBLISHING *HAPPY MANIA*—WHICH CHARTS THE ROMANTIC MISADVENTURES OF PROTAGONIST SHIGETA— IN THE JOSEI MAGAZINE *FEEL YOUNG*; IT WAS AN OVERWHELMING SUCCESS. THE FEMALE CHARACTERS IN HER WORK ARE COMPLEX AND MULTIFACETED, WHETHER THEY'RE WOMEN IN CONTEMPORARY JAPANESE SOCIETY (*IN CLOTHES CALLED FAT, HATARAKI MAN*), OR HISTORICAL SETTINGS (*SAKURAN, MEMOIRS OF AMOROUS GENTLEMEN*.) HER STORIES HAVE TOUCHED THE HEARTS AND AMPLIFIED THE VOICES OF MANY YOUNG JAPANESE WOMEN.

FUN FACT
ANNO HAS A PASSION FOR FASHION, AND LAUNCHED HER OWN BRAND OF KIMONO IN 2020.

6

CULT SERIES

By now you've seen how integral the artwork, story structure, and character development are to a manga's success. The series I'll tell you about over the next few pages are exemplary in every way: I would recommend them all as wonderful sources of inspiration for your own stories.
I hope you love them as much as I—and many other manga fans—do too!

DEATH NOTE AND BAKUMAN: MANGA AS COLLABORATION

THERE IS ONE PARTNERSHIP—THAT OF WRITER TSUGUMI OHBA AND ILLUSTRATOR TAKESHI OBATA—THAT HAS HAD A HUGE IMPACT ON THE HISTORY OF MANGA.

GOOD LUCK WITH THE SCHOOL PLAY, JUDY!

DEATH NOTE, WHICH WAS PUBLISHED IN *SHŌNEN JUMP* FROM 2003 TO 2006, IS A PSYCHOLOGICAL THRILLER WITH SUPERNATURAL ELEMENTS. IT TELLS THE STORY OF THE CLASH BETWEEN LIGHT YAGAMI—A MODEL STUDENT WHO TAKES THE LAW INTO HIS OWN HANDS—AND L, A GENIUS DETECTIVE WHO IS INTENT ON SOLVING THE MYSTERIOUS, UNEXPLAINED DEATHS OF CRIMINALS.

YEAH. BREAK A LEG JUDY SMITH . . .

THE DEATH NOTE IS THE NOTEBOOK IN WHICH THE **SHINIGAMI**—THE GODS OF DEATH IN JAPANESE CULTURE— WRITE THE NAMES OF THE PEOPLE WHO ARE TO BE CARRIED OFF INTO THE AFTERLIFE. IN THE MANGA, LIGHT YAGAMI GETS HIS HANDS ON A LOST DEATH NOTE AND DECIDES TO RID THE WORLD OF INJUSTICE. HE BECOMES A VIGILANTE WHO DISHES OUT HIS OWN ROUGH JUSTICE, WRITING IN THE NOTEBOOK THE NAMES OF ALL THE BAD PEOPLE HE THINKS DESERVE TO DIE. THE SERIES IS A MEDITATION ON THE ETERNAL STRUGGLE BETWEEN GOOD AND EVIL. RICH IN UNEXPECTED PLOT TWISTS, IT CHALLENGES EVERY READER'S IDEA OF JUSTICE.

BAKUMAN WAS CREATED BY THE SAME TEAM BEHIND *DEATH NOTE*
AND PUBLISHED IN *SHŌNEN JUMP* FROM 2008 TO 2012.
IT'S A MANGA ABOUT MANGA, WHICH TELLS THE STORY OF TWO TEENAGE
CLASSMATES, AKITO AND MORITAKA, WHO BOTH DREAM OF BECOMING MANGAKA
AND SEEING ONE OF THEIR CREATIONS MADE INTO AN ANIME.
THROUGH ITS ACCURATE DEPICTION OF THE JAPANESE PUBLISHING WORLD, IT REVEALS
HOW THE COMIC BOOK INDUSTRY WORKS, HOW A MANGA IS ADAPTED INTO AN ANIME,
AND EVEN EXPLORES THE WORLD OF ANIME VOICE-ACTING.

BAKUMAN ALSO CONTAINS A NUMBER OF FICTIONAL COMICS, WRITTEN AND ILLUSTRATED
BY THE CHARACTERS IN THE STORY. SOME OF THESE PROVED SO POPULAR
THEY BECAME MANGA IN THEIR OWN RIGHT!

WE COULD BE
THE NEW TSUGUMI OHBA
AND TAKESHI OBATA!

HM . . . WHO WOULD WRITE
AND WHO WOULD DRAW?

IN THE FIRST 20 YEARS OF THE 2000S, THE MANGA LANDSCAPE WAS DOMINATED BY THREE BATTLE SHŌNEN: THESE TITLES HAVE CAPTURED THE HEARTS AND MINDS OF READERS ALL OVER THE WORLD, AND HAVE SOLD MILLIONS OF COPIES.

ONE PIECE BY EIICHIRŌ ODA HAS BEEN PUBLISHED IN *SHŌNEN JUMP* SINCE 1997. WITH OVER 100 PUBLISHED VOLUMES TO ITS NAME, AS WELL AS MORE THAN 1000 ANIME EPISODES AND AN INTERNATIONALLY ACCLAIMED LIVE ACTION SERIES RELEASED ON NETFLIX IN 2023, IT REALLY IS THE KING OF MANGA. SET IN A WORLD LARGELY COVERED BY SEAS, WHERE THE WORLD GOVERNMENT CONTROLS THE FEW AREAS OF DRY LAND AND ITS NAVY HUNTS DOWN PIRATES, THE STORY FOLLOWS THE ADVENTURES OF MONKEY D. LUFFY AND HIS CREW AS THEY SEARCH FOR THE MOST COVETED TREASURE IN THE WORLD, THE "ONE PIECE" THAT ONCE BELONGED TO THE PIRATE KING GOL D. ROGER.

ODA'S SKILFUL COMMAND OF HIS MATERIAL, AND ITS ORIGINALITY, DRAWS THE READER INTO A COLORFUL, COMPELLING, AND EMOTIONALLY RICH WORLD OF ADVENTURES. THE STORY IS A HYMN TO FREEDOM IN THE FACE OF TYRANNY, CORRUPTION, AND DISCRIMINATION.

I'M SURE WE'LL FIND OUR OWN ONE PIECE!

NARUTO BY MASASHI KISHIMOTO WAS PUBLISHED IN *SHŌNEN JUMP* FROM 1999 TO 2014. THE SERIES IS MADE UP OF 72 TANKŌBONS AND IT IS ONE OF THE MOST POPULAR SHŌNEN SAGAS IN THE WORLD. IT TELLS THE STORY OF NARUTO UZUMAKI, A YOUNG NINJA FROM HIDDEN LEAF VILLAGE WHO HAS BEEN CAST OUT BY HIS COMMUNITY BECAUSE OF A TERRIBLE CURSE THAT HANGS OVER HIM. HE DREAMS OF EARNING THE VILLAGE'S RESPECT AND BEING CHOSEN FOR ITS HIGHEST OFFICE AS THE **HOKAGE**, OR LEADER.

BY COMBINING ASPECTS OF CHINESE AND JAPANESE CULTURE AND MYTHOLOGY WITH CONFUCIANISM, KISHIMOTO CREATED A STORY WITH UNIVERSAL VALUES: *NARUTO* IS A TRIBUTE TO THE IMPORTANCE OF LOYALTY AND FRIENDSHIP, AND THE VIRTUES OF COMMITMENT AND PERSEVERANCE.

SEVENTY-FOUR VOLUMES OF *BLEACH* BY TITE KUBO WERE PUBLISHED IN *SHŌNEN JUMP* FROM 2001 TO 2016, AND THANKS TO ITS MEMORABLE CHARACTERS, DYNAMIC FIGHT SCENES, AND SOPHISTICATED ART STYLE, THE SERIES EARNED MILLIONS OF READERS. THE STORY FOLLOWS THE ADVENTURES OF ICHIGO KUROSAKI, A STUDENT WHO GAINS THE SKILLS OF A SHINIGAMI. AS A RESULT, THE BOY FINDS HIMSELF IN THE SOUL SOCIETY, THE PLACE WHERE THE SOULS OF THE DEAD GO, AND IS TASKED WITH MAINTAINING THE DELICATE BALANCE BETWEEN THE KINGDOMS OF LIFE AND DEATH.

IF WE'RE GOING TO WORK AS A TEAM, WE HAVE TO TRUST EACH OTHER . . .

20ᵀᴴ CENTURY BOYS WAS PUBLISHED IN *BIG COMIC SPIRITS* MAGAZINE FROM 1999 TO 2006, AND IS ONE OF NAOKI UROSAWA'S MOST RECOGNIZABLE WORKS. UROSAWA IS AMONG THE MOST SIGNIFICANT *SEINEN* MANGA ARTISTS ALIVE TODAY AND HAS WON COUNTLESS AWARDS, INCLUDING THE EISNER AWARD. THE STORY OF *20ᵀᴴ CENTURY BOYS* FOLLOWS THE CHARACTER OF KENJI ENDO ACROSS TWO TIME PERIODS. THE FIRST, IN 1969, FOCUSES ON KENJI'S CHILDHOOD, HIS FRIENDS, AND THE AFTERNOONS THEY SPEND IN THEIR SECRET HIDEOUT. THE BOYS IMAGINE A FUTURE IN WHICH THEY FIGHT FOR THE GOOD OF THE EARTH AS MEMBERS OF AN ORGANIZATION THEY INVENTED, WHOSE LOGO IS A HAND POINTING TOWARDS AN EYE.

THE SECOND PART OF THE STORY TAKES PLACE IN 1997, AND FINDS KENJI INVESTIGATING THE CRIMES COMMITTED BY A CULT WHO USE THE EXACT SAME LOGO DREAMED UP BY HIMSELF AND HIS FRIENDS AS CHILDREN. URASAWA'S MANGA COMPARES TWO VERY DIFFERENT JAPANS: THE COUNTRY AT THE END OF THE 1960S, CHARACTERIZED BY HOPE, AND FAITH IN THE FUTURE; AND THE ONE AT THE END OF THE 1990S, MARKED BY DISILLUSIONMENT, THE ECONOMIC RECESSION, AND A FEAR OF CULTS FOLLOWING THE 1995 TERRORIST ATTACK ON THE TOKYO SUBWAY.

BOYS' LOVE

THE ORIGINS OF THE BOYS' LOVE GENRE GO BACK TO THE 1970S AND ARE ROOTED IN MANGA LIKE *THE HEART OF THOMAS* BY HAGIO MOTO AND *THE POEM OF WIND AND TREES* BY KEIKO TAKEMIYA. BOTH MANGA ARE SET IN EUROPE, AND DEPICT LOVE STORIES BETWEEN TEENAGE BOYS. WRITING LOVE STORIES WITH MALE CHARACTERS IN THE SHŌJO GENRE ALLOWED MANY FEMALE MANGA ARTISTS AND READERS TO EXPLORE DESIRE, SEXUALITY, AND OTHER TABOO SUBJECTS AT A TIME WHEN IT WAS LESS ACCEPTED FOR WOMEN TO DO SO THROUGH A FEMININE PERSPECTIVE.

TODAY THE TERM "BOYS' LOVE" INCLUDES A WIDE RANGE OF TITLES, WHICH CAN HAVE DIFFERENT PLOTS, SETTINGS, AND SUB-GENRES OF THEIR OWN. THESE MANGA TEND TO BE WRITTEN BY WOMEN AND ARE GENERALLY AIMED AT FEMALE READERS. *OUR NOT-SO-LONELY PLANET TRAVEL GUIDE* BY MONE SORAI, FOR EXAMPLE, TELLS THE STORY OF PROTAGONISTS ASAHI AND MITSUKI AS THEY TRAVEL AROUND THE WORLD TOGETHER, HAVING MADE A PACT THAT THEY CAN'T GET MARRIED UNTIL THEY HAVE GONE ALL THE WAY AROUND THE GLOBE.

THE TWO OF US ARE ONE! I'LL SUPPORT YOU, AND YOU CAN SUPPORT ME! THAT IS OUR GREATEST STRENGTH.

DORAEMON IS ONE OF THE MOST ICONIC AND POPULAR CHARACTERS TO HAVE COME OUT OF JAPAN. AS A KEY FIGURE IN THE SPREAD OF JAPANESE CULTURE AROUND THE WORLD, THE CHARACTER WAS EVEN GIVEN THE TITLE OF "ANIME AMBASSADOR" BY THE JAPANESE FOREIGN MINISTER! WRITTEN AND ILLUSTRATED BY FUJIKO F. FUJIO AND SERIALIZED BETWEEN 1969 AND 1997 IN A VARIETY OF CHILDREN'S MAGAZINES PUBLISHED BY SHOGAKUKAN, *DORAEMON* BELONGS TO THE KODOMO GAG-MANGA GENRE, BUT ALSO FEATURES ELEMENTS OF SCIENCE FICTION.

MORE THAN 1300 CHAPTERS WERE PUBLISHED OVER A 30-YEAR PERIOD! ITS EPISODIC STRUCTURE RECOUNTS THE DAILY ADVENTURES OF NOBITA, A BORED LITTLE BOY WHO ISN'T GOOD AT ANYTHING; AND DORAEMON, A ROBOT CAT FROM THE TWENTY-SECOND CENTURY. EVERY CHAPTER SEES DORAEMON TRYING TO HELP NOBITA BY OFFERING HIM MIRACULOUS OBJECTS FROM THE FUTURE THAT COULD SOLVE THE BOY'S PROBLEMS. YET NOBITA ALWAYS ENDS UP MISUSING THE OBJECTS, CAUSING THEIR EFFECTS TO BACKFIRE . . . BUT TEACHING HIM A VALUABLE LIFE LESSON.

DO YOU THINK THAT'S A ROBOT CAT FROM THE FUTURE? IT COULD JOIN OUR TEAM . . .

MAYBE IT CAN TELL US ABOUT OUR FUTURE BESTSELLERS . . .

ONE PUNCH MAN AND THE FUTURE OF MANGA

AMONG THE MOST IMPORTANT MANGA OF RECENT YEARS,
YOU COULD UNDOUBTEDLY LIST *MY HERO ACADEMIA*, *DEMON SLAYER*,
HAIKYU!!, AND *ATTACK ON TITAN*. BUT MORE THAN ANY OTHER, ONE TITLE
IN PARTICULAR SEEMS TO EXEMPLIFY HOW THE WORLD OF MANGA
HAS CHANGED IN THE NEW MILLENNIUM: *ONE-PUNCH MAN*.
ONE-PUNCH MAN BEGAN IN 2009 AS A WEB-MANGA
CREATED BY A SINGLE AUTHOR, ONE, WHO WAS FAMOUS
FOR HIS VERY SIMPLE DRAWING STYLE.
ONE-PUNCH MAN IS A GAG MANGA THAT PARODIES
THE CONVENTIONAL FEATURES OF SHŌNEN, SUCH AS
THE HERO'S JOURNEY OF GROWTH AND SELF-DISCOVERY
ACHIEVED THROUGH SACRIFICE AND DETERMINATION.
ITS MAIN CHARACTER, SAITAMA, IS SO STRONG THAT HE CAN DEFEAT
ANY OPPONENT EASILY WITH A SINGLE PUNCH.
THE MANGA IMMEDIATELY WENT VIRAL AND HAS BEEN
A HUGE SUCCESS IN JAPAN.

WE DON'T NEED HELP FROM THE FUTURE!

WE'LL MAKE THE MANGA OF THE FUTURE!

IN 2012, THE ONLINE PLATFORM *TONARI NO YOUNG JUMP*
(LINKED TO THE MAGAZINE OF THE SAME NAME) LAUNCHED
WITH A REMAKE OF ONE'S MANGA, THIS TIME WITH DRAWINGS
BY YUSUKE MURATA, WHO HAD ALREADY MADE HIS NAME WITH
THE *EYESHIELD 21* SERIES. THIS IS THE VERSION THAT ACHIEVED
WORLDWIDE SUCCESS OUTSIDE OF JAPAN.
ONE PUNCH MAN IS A STRIKING EXAMPLE OF A MANGA THAT HAS
GROWN WITH DIGITAL TECHNOLOGY AND USED IT TO ITS ADVANTAGE.
AFTER FIRST APPEARING ONLINE, IT FOUND FURTHER SUCCESS
IN A NEW VERSION—ALSO PUBLISHED DIGITALLY—BEFORE BEING
SERIALIZED IN PRINT ALL OVER THE WORLD. AS MANGA ARTISTS,
WE HAVE TO BE AWARE OF HOW THE WORLD IS CHANGING,
AND HOW COMICS MUST ADAPT TO MAINTAIN THEIR RELEVANCE
AND POPULARITY.

▶ RECOMMENDED READING

Panel 1: "HOW COME WHENEVER I'M WITH YOU WE END UP HERE?"

"WAIT, I'VE GOT SOMETHING TO SHOW YOU . . ."

Panel 2: "WHAT'S THAT IN YOUR HAND?!"

"THE LIST!"

Panel 3: "WH . . . WHA . . . WHAT LIST?"

"WHAT DO YOU MEAN? THE LIST WITH ALL THE BAD PEOPLE TO BE WIPED OFF THE FACE OF THE EARTH!"

Panel 4: "GULP!"

"I'M JOKING! COME ON, SCAREDY CAT."

Panel 5: "IT'S ALL THE BOOKS FUMIO AND MY MOM RECOMMENDED WE READ!"

"OHHHHH . . ."

Panel 6: "WELL—I KNOW WHERE ALL MY MONEY'S GOING!"

MUST-READ MANGA!

20TH CENTURY BOYS—NAOKI URASAWA
A DRIFTING LIFE—YOSHIHIRO TATSUMI
A SILENT VOICE—YOSHITOKI OIMA
ASTRO BOY—OSAMU TEZUKA
ATTACK ON TITAN—HAJIME ISAYAMA
BAKUMAN—TSUGUMI OHBA & TAKESHI OBATA
BERSERK—KENTARO MIURA
BLACK JACK—OSAMU TEZUKA
BLAME—TSUTOMU NIHEI
BLEACH—TITE KUBO
BLUE PERIOD—TSUBASA YAMAGUCHI
CAPTAIN TSUBASA—YOICHI TAKAHASHI
CARD CAPTOR SAKURA—CLAMP
CASE CLOSED—GOSHO AOYAMA
CAT'S EYE—TSUKASA HOJO
CITY HUNTER—TSUKASA HOJO
DEATH NOTE—TSUGUMI OHBA & TAKESHI OBATA
DEMON SLAYER—KOYOHARU GOTOUGE
DEVILMAN—GO NAGAI
DORAEMON—FUJIKO F. FUJIO
DR. STONE—RIICHIRO INAGAKI & BOICHI
DR. SLUMP—AKIRA TORIYAMA
DRAGON BALL—AKIRA TORIYAMA
ENDO—PEPPE
ST OF THE NORTH STAR—BURONSON & TETSUO HARA

FOOD WARS—YUTO TSUKUDA & SHUN SAEKI
HAIKYU!!—HARUICHI FURUDATE
HAPPY MANIA—MOYOCO ANNO
HELTER SKELTER—KYOKO OKAZAKI
HOKUSAI MANGA—HOKUSAI
HUNTER X HUNTER—YOSHIHIRO TOGASHI
INUYASHA—RUMIKO TAKAHASHI
JOJO'S BIZARRE ADVENTURE—HIROHIKO ARAKI
JUST SO HAPPENS—FUMIO OBATA
KIMBA THE WHITE LION—OSAMU TEZUKA
MAZINGER Z—GO NAGAI
MY BROTHER'S HUSBAND—GENGOROH TAGAME
MY HERO ACADEMIA—KOHEI HORIKOSHI
NANA—AI YAZAWA
NARUTO—MASASHI KISHIMOTO
ONE PIECE—EIICHIRO ODA
ONE PUNCH MAN—ONE & YUSUKE MURATA
OUR NOT-SO-LONELY PLANET TRAVEL GUIDE—MONE SORAI
PARADISE KISS—AI YAZAWA
RADIANT—TONY VALENTE
SAILOR MOON—NAOKO TAKEUCHI
SAINT SEIYA—MASAMI KURUMADA
SEVEN DEADLY SINS—NAKABA SUZUKI
SLAM DUNK—TAKEHIKO INOUE
THE HEART OF THOMAS—MOTO HAGIO
THE ROSE OF VERSAILLES—RIYOKO IKEDA
TOKYO GHOUL—SUI ISHIDA
TOMIE—JUNJI ITO
UZUMAKI—JUNJI ITO
VAGABOND—TAKEHIKO INOUE
YU GI OH—KAZUKI TAKAHASHI

GLOSSARY

Anime: アニメ, animations for film or television made in Japan.

Bishōjo: 美少女, "beautiful girl," in manga a female character designed with "cute" and feminine characteristics.

Bishōnen : 美少年, "beautiful boy," in manga a male character designed with androgynous characteristics.

Dōjinshi: 同人誌, a self-published work of fan-fiction, typically a magazine or manga, based on a pre-existing work and distributed at conventions and specialist bookstores.

E-maki: 絵巻, stories told with words and illustrations printed on scrolls, a precursor to manga.

Gakuen: 学園, school or academy, also used to describe a genre of manga with a school or academy as the main setting.

Gekiga: 劇画, literally "dramatic pictures," a term referring to a manga style popular in the 1960s and 70s, featuring stories with more mature themes, darker tones, and art styles more targeted to an adult audience.

Genkō yōshi: 原稿用紙, "manuscript paper." Special "manga genkō yōshi" have specific guidelines for creating the standard dimensions of manga pages.

Hetare: ヘタレ, a cowardly or unconfident character type found in manga.

Isekai: 異世界, literally "another world," referring to a genre in which a protagonist is transported from their home (typically the modern-day) to another world (typically with a fantasy or video-game style setting).

Josei: 女性, manga aimed at adult women readers, exploring adult topics such as work and relationships.

Kanji: 漢字, Japanese writing system that adapts Chinese characters.

Ki-sho-ten-ketsu: 起承転結, "start – follow – turn/climax – end," a four-step story-crafting model that is the basis for the Eastern storytelling.

Kodomo: 子供, manga aimed at young children, often episodic and with a moral lesson.

Komawari: コマ割り, the layout and flow of panels on the page of a manga, and the process of planning them out.

Mahō shōjo: 魔法少女, "magical girl," a term referring to the subgenre of manga about girls with magical powers fighting against evil, also known as majokko.

Manga: 漫画, literally "whimsical pictures," the Japanese word generally used for comics in Japan, while internationally the term is used for comics created in Japan.

Mangaka: 漫画家, the artist and/or writer who creates a manga.

Mochikomi: 持ち込み, literally "bring-your-own," the practice of submitting an unpublished manga to an editor for feedback and for potential publication.

Name: ネーム, a provisional draft format used to plan out pages of a manga, such as speech bubble placement.

Ponchi-E: ポンチ絵, derived from the English *Punch* newspaper, single-panel satirical cartoons published in Japanese newspapers, a precursor to manga.

Seinen: 青年, manga aimed at young adult male readers, featuring mature themes and an emphasis on plot and characters.

Shinigami: 死神, the "kami" or deities of death from Japanese mythology. Shinigami feature as characters in prominent manga such as *Death Note* and *Bleach*.

Shōjo : 少女, manga aimed at pre-teen to teenage female readers.

Shōnen: 少年, manga aimed at pre-teen to teenage male readers.

Shonen Ai: 少年愛, "Boys' Love," a genre of manga depicting a romantic relationship between two male characters.

Spokon: スポ根, combination of the English "sports" and the Japanese "konjō" (meaning tenacity, persistence.)

Tankōbon: 単行本, literally "independent book," a format of manga publication for either a single, standalone work or a collection of chapters of an ongoing manga series.

Tokusatsu: 特撮 – literally "special effects," a term referring to live action tv shows or films that use extensive practical special effects.

Yonkoma: 四コマ, a four-panel illustrated comic with a self-contained, usually humorous story.

INDEX